The Liquid Accordion

*A Somatic and Embodiment Primer
for Coaching In, With, and Through
the Body for Coaches and Leaders*

Croft Edwards, MCC

Clovercroft Publishing

The Liquid Accordion: A Somatic and Embodiment Primer for Coaching In, With, and Through the Body for Coaches and Leaders
©2026 by Croft Edwards

Published by Clovercroft Publishing, Franklin, Tennessee

Edited by Robert Irvin

Cover and Interior Design by Suzanne Lawing

Images by the author and Mirza Zahid

Printed in PRC

ISBN: (print) 978-1-968127-15-2

Contents

Part 1

The WHY of Coaching In, With, and Through the Body

Part 2

The WHAT and WHERE of Coaching In, With, and Through the Body

Part 3
The HOW of Coaching In, With, and Through the Body

Preface

Little did I know that one day I would be writing a book about coaching in, with, and through the body. After all, for a large part of my life I was blind to my body and how it affected and created the world I lived in. Like many, I was simply a brain on a stick. My world was, as I saw it, how the world was. After all, it was so clear to me how things were. There were things in the world which were right and things which were wrong. The world was black, the world was white, and occasionally there was gray. This viewpoint, for the most part, served me, leading me through college and my start of a career as a military officer. That was to change, slowly at first, but it was to change.

After I had left active duty of five years in the US Army, I had somewhat followed my passion of studying leadership and had evolved into a semi-competent leadership consultant and performance coach. I had been working for a leadership-and-change, coaching-and-consulting firm for about four years. For the majority of the time I was "coaching" (i.e., telling people what to do) in a project with a large palladium and platinum mine in the western US. I had grown quite smug and heady in my abilities and, because of the scope of the work, I had accumulated more than six hundred hours of actual coaching and decided I wanted to get the prestigious International Coaching Federation (ICF) Professional Certified Coach (PCC) designation. To qualify for the designation I needed to have the requisite 750 hours of actual coaching, which I would have in less than a year. Additionally, I needed 125 hours of coach-specific training, which in my mind was simply a check-the-box issue as I was sure there was not much I could yet learn about coaching.

Luckily, as fate would have it, I stumbled into the Newfield Network. In that year, 2004, Newfield was heading up a leadership and coaching program being held jointly with the Villanova University Department of Executive Education. The program was a great fit for me as I was then in the Army Reserve, and because the program fell across two fiscal years the Army would pick up the tab as professional development education for me for both years. This would work great for me; all I really needed to do was show up, take a few notes, and then breeze down the path of getting my PCC designation.

In reality, my world was about to be rocked.

I showed up the first day of the program with my usual armored-up body and wearing my mask of leadership as I walked into the room. My body was tense, but having practiced being in difficult situations before, and having years of conditioning my body to be numbed for potential combat, I was ready. I walked into the medium-sized ballroom and my body immediately tensed up even more. As I scanned the potential battlefield with my squinty and hardened face I was immediately thrown off by all the giggling and laughing and soft and loving niceness everywhere. There were people who seemed to be really open and vulnerable and, quite frankly, were too open and too vulnerable for me. After all, we were here to talk about leadership, and I was a US Army Captain, part of the organization that owned the rights to the title of *leadership*. Nonetheless, I figured I could make it through three long weekends with these people. After all, I had a goal to accomplish, and I had spent a year deployed in a potential combat zone in the Army, so how hard could this be?

On the afternoon of the first day, after lunch, we participated in the first somatic portion of the course. My initial thought: *semantics? What does word usage have to do with leadership and coaching?* After I realized the word was somatic, a word which I did not have a meaning for, it was too late—we were already moving. The somatic portion was led by a masterful coach, Curtis Watkins, who, I assessed, must have some knowledge of what he was doing. I am not really sure what we did in the first class; my mind only remembers dancing and feeling really uncomfortable. I have this vision of me walking around like a soldier in combat while fairies and leprechauns danced around me. My only solace was that there seemed to be many others in the room who had the same look of *What the f#$%^ are we doing?* And so, somehow, I made it through that first session. As weird as the first day seemed, I was committed to the program; it was a necessary step to my PCC designation and, quite frankly, it was going to be easier to finish the program than to navigate the Army red tape should I not do so.

Day two showed up and I was ready to face the gauntlet again, although I realized some of my *What the F#$%^?* comrades did not make it through the night. It was late in the morning on the second day when Julio Olalla, the founder of the Newfield Network and one of the founding fathers of ontological coaching, was speaking. He was simply being Julio, completely entrancing the audience with his guru-like presence and eloquence when I suddenly became aware that my body was numb. It was not numb like it could not feel, but rather it was numb like it *could* feel. There was a tingling throughout my body and a peaceful "aliveness" washing over me. I remember thinking to myself: *there is something here.* I was not sure what it was, but there was something which said, throughout my body: *you are safe and you are in the right place.*

That afternoon's somatic session was different for me. It was as if my stiff, armored body had, for the first time in years, been loosened up. It was not so heavy, it was not so tense. It was the first time I think I ever truly realized I *had* a body . . .

* * * * * * *

What started at Newfield so many years ago has led me to this book. After graduating the course, getting my PCC designation, and a few more years of practicing ontological coaching, I became a mentor coach for Newfield in the US. A few years later I became a mentor coach for what was then Newfield Network Asia (now the Coach Partnership). I continued my ontological learning and found myself truly drawn to somatic learning. I completed the Institute of Generative Leadership (IGL) Coaching Excellence in Organizations, a three-year, graduate-level program and spent a large amount of time with the Strozzi Institute, the premier somatic coaching learning organization. Then, for several years, I worked as a mentor coach in their Somatic Coaching Program and the Strozzi Institute Teacher Training.

As I look back on my evolution as a coach, I went from being blind to the body, not even aware of it in coaching either in myself or my coachees, to now many, if not most, of my coaching relationships having some sort of somatic coaching component. Many of the coaching conversations I'm now in are somatic coaching relationships, and we spend large amounts of time exploring how the coachee shows up, somatically, in the world.

That being said, I am obviously an advocate and proponent of coaching in, with, and through the body. In my many coaching relationships where I am the mentor coach, the subject of somatic coaching comes up, and invariably the coachee asks for more references on coaching and, specifically, somatic coaching. I have shared many of what I consider well-written and powerful coaching and ontological coaching resources with my coachees. What I have not been able to share with them is a place to start to explore somatics or the body. I do not know of any books which are simply a foundational somatic starting point.

There are many good books written about somatics, but I assess that they have two major deficiencies in their content. The first is that they are written at a very high level and, in a sense, theoretical. They do not have some basic first steps for the reader as how to coach in, with, and through the body. The other challenge is that all of the books in the field that I have come across assume the reader has some fundamental grounding in somatics and coaching in the body. There seems to be a missing piece to the somatic coaching puzzle—that being a baseline, foundational book on coaching in, with, and through the body. That is the goal of this book.

Foreword

My life – and the trajectory of my life – changed dramatically starting in 1987. Little did I know that attending a weekend workshop – under the relentless "encouragement" of some friends who had previously attended – would forever shift how I saw myself and my possibilities, how I thought about and related to other people, and ultimately the contribution I wanted to make in the world. The little company was called Education for Living and it was our introduction to the world of ontological coaching. A bit more on exactly what's included here is coming, but for now I'd like to say that it shook my "terminal certainty" about "the way things are!"

We attended a few more programs in Louisiana over the next couple of years, and it was clear by then that I had found something that resonated with me in a way that I'd never experienced before. I ultimately found my way to the Newfield Network, and in 1995 completed the yearlong program Mastering the Art of Professional Coaching. While the programs with Education for Living were giving us the experience of *being coached,* the Newfield Network program was (and is) a program designed to also *certify coaches…* and more specifically, to certify ontological coaches.

Since January, 1996, this body of learning has been the central focus of my professional life – all I have been doing since then is 1) creating and speaking and delivering programs based on my version of what I've learned; 2) writing two books intended to share as widely as I can the things that have been most impactful and beneficial to me; and 3) providing personal and executive coaching using these same distinctions, tools, practices and "ways of seeing things."

At the heart of this body of learning are a few basic, fundamental claims that may at first seem obvious, but once they're adopted and embraced, an entirely new world of possibilities opens up. The first one is this: You and I and everyone we have ever known and ever will know may be understood as walking, talking bundles of congruency and coherency that include three distinct yet highly interrelated domains:

- Our language (internal and external conversations)

- Our moods and emotions

- Our physical bodies and biology

Said another way, the unique combination of these three domains that = you… and that = me… and that = every other person… may be understood as our Way of Being. This includes our ways of walking, talking, thinking, emoting, breathing, sitting, standing, relating… as well as all of the "internal" biological processes that happen totally unnoticed by us… all of it. And any one of these three primary domains may be the "leverage" point or starting point for change, for shifting and for bringing about a new and different Way of Being.

At a basic level, virtually all of us have experienced feeling better (which is mood) after exercising (which is body). And when we're in a mood of ambition, for example, do we not then interpret (which is language) the same objective event differently that we would've had we been in a mood of resentment?

Needless to say, I had gone through my first 36 years on the planet and never heard anyone talk about a Way of Being and never really thought about my particular Way of Being.

Understanding the interdependency and interrelatedness of these three domains… and learning new distinctions that allow us to literally see what we couldn't see before… open the door to the possibility of new practices that can dramatically transform our Way of Being. And this is crucially important to understand: From our Way of Being… from how we "are" and how we "see things"… we take Action in the world. And from the Actions we take in the world, we produce Results in the world – in a wide, wide variety of areas, professionally and personally, objective Results and subjective Results, quantitative Results and qualitative Results.

My books are titled *Language and the Pursuit of Happiness* (2005) and *Language and the Pursuit of Leadership Excellence* (2015). Guess which of the three domains I focused on and gravitated to? Obviously, language.

In some ways, this focus for me mirrored my life in that I had lived my life up until that point – with the possible exception of my days playing baseball and football – not even thinking about or paying much attention to or considering my body. Like a lot of people, I think my orientation was basically that I was a "head on a stick," and whatever my body was doing was pretty much irrelevant… the main thing was the ways I was thinking and talking and engaging and relating, not so much at all about the actual physical structure that "housed" and enabled the thinking, talking, engaging and relating to begin with!

Croft Edwards and I crossed paths beginning back in 2012, as he was also a Newfield Network certified coach, was interested in leadership and was doing workshops, training and coaching based on the same body of work. Over the years we have shared ideas, thoughts and experiences having to do with many of the different ways that these tools and ways of understanding can be applied regarding leadership and within organizations of all sizes and shapes – as well as with people at all stages of their lives. As fellow authors working within the same broad body of learning, I've learned a lot from Croft; I've really enjoyed the collaborative nature of our relationship and have recommended Croft and his work regularly over the years.

I am thrilled and honored to be part of Croft's new contribution, as I believe it fills a major gap, a major void. While there are a great many outstanding books – written by tremendously talented, insightful, skilled practitioners and writers – that have to do with the body, I have not found one that does what Liquid Accordion does. To me, this new book:

- Serves as a genuine primer, a very accessible and practical starting point for people at all levels who are seeking to learn more about the ways in which the body they already have has historically been influencing their emotional life as well as their ways of thinking and interpreting... as well as ways their emotional life and ways of thinking and interpreting have been influencing and impacting their body;

- Provides easy to understand frameworks, empowering new distinctions and helpful practices that all of us can adopt – immediately – in order to more effectively leverage the interdependency inherent among our physical bodies and biology, our moods and emotions and our internal and external conversations;

- Teaches us how to better take care of ourselves and the people we care about on multiple levels – whether we are coming to this book as a practicing coach, a leader or manager, a parent, a partner or simply a human being seeking new ways of understanding who we are and some of the most important and helpful aspects and characteristics and possibilities that are embodied within each of us.

In the pages that follow you'll learn (or remember!) Why our bodies are absolutely worth exploring in this way, absolutely worth the effort to deepen our understanding here.

You'll also learn What is involved in this sort of exploration, what key aspects or dimensions or elements are most important... what they do, how they function and the ways in which they interact and are inter-related.

And you'll also learn How to use your new awareness and understanding in order to bring about genuine shifts and improvements in your well-being and the well-being of others, as well as in virtually any situations in which people are working together, living together, playing together... *being* together.

I am glad you have picked up this book, and can confidently say that it can be both a wonderful starting point as well as a very practical "owners manual" for yourself starting today and continuing through the months and years ahead.

Wishing you well on all fronts, and remember: never stop learning!

Chalmers Brothers
Naples, Florida
July 20, 2025

Acknowledgments

The journey of this book has been a long one, with the actual writing taking over five years on and off. The journey of my understanding of the body as a place of knowledge has been evolving for at least over 20 years. There are many who I should and want to thank. There are also many who, although their names do not appear in this writing, added to the mix and DNA of this book with conversations, both on the subject of somatic coaching and coaching in general. There are also literally hundreds and hundreds of my coachee's over the years who in our conversations allowed me to be a practitioner of Somatic Coaching. For those not listed, but who contributed to this work, I sincerely thank you. If you assess a bit of disappointment at not being listed I truly and sincerely apologize for the oversight.

There are those that I assess I must address here to thank you for your wisdom, love, feedback, friendship in this journey to bring this book to print.

For all of my fellow coaches who helped in this journey. Thank you for all of your insights, inspiration and teachings. I appreciate you. Specifically, in no particular order, Carol Courcey, Tini Fadzillah, MCC, Lisa Collins, MCC, Laura McCafferty, MCC, Chris Balsley, PCC, Amanda Duarte, PCC, Bob Dunham, Chalmers Brothers, Julio Olalla. If your name is not shown here and you added something, I apologize for the oversight; this journey took much longer than I anticipated and unfortunately a few things might have dropped.

To Bob Irvin, Shane Crabtree, Suzanne Lawing and the team at Clovercroft Publishing, a sincere thanks. Bob, your editing wisdom, direct feedback, and sincere care are truly appreciated. You allowed my voice to shine through and helped to focus and clarify my writing; I thank you. Shane, thanks for navigating the path forward. Suzanne, thank you for bringing it all together in a coherent and powerful package. Also, I so appreciate the book cover!

To Mirza Zahid, my graphic designer who brought both the *Liquid Accordion* character and the human models alive. You worked tirelessly and were a joy to work with. Your patience with the many revisions and sometimes confusing directions from me had to be a challenge and yet you never showed it. The images are all I wanted and more. I thank you.

To my sister and former teammate Mary Kay Gibbs, thank you for all you have done and do in my life, I truly appreciate it. I am so grateful that you are such a role model for my daughters. Keep being you. We all love you dearly.

For the four foundational women in my life. You all inspire me. Thank you, Jeanne, for creating a world where we all thrive, you are the best and I love you. To my three beautiful daughters, Sophie, Olivia, and Ana, you are now spreading your wings and flying the nest. I love you all and look forward to your journeys.

· · · · · · · · · · · · · · · · · ·

Dedications

To Curtis Watkins: my first somatic teacher—I never thanked you for opening the door to somatics and my awareness of the body. Your legacy lives on in the future coaches of this lineage. Thank you!

To Richard Strozzi-Heckler: for embodying the ability to walk in diverse worlds. Thank you for opening the path!

To Gary Gibbs: a brother-in-law, friend, mentor. You helped me to find my strength in the gym, and my center in our conversations. — GATA

To Marc Smith-Sacks: a true friend, a masterful coach; you will be missed. You mastered your body, climbed mountains, and left those who loved you with a desire to live the good life!

Who Needs This Book–and Why

What is the likely reason you are picking up this book? My guess is there is one of four reasons you have this book in front of you.

1) You are a beginner coach who is enrolled in, or has just completed, a coach training program with an ontological/somatic-based training organization. In the program you learned some fundamental body/somatic distinctions and might be curious and desiring to take your learning about coaching in, with, or through the body deeper. This book is for you.

2) You are a more established coach in a transformational coaching discipline and have some knowledge of coaching in, with, and through the body. You are ready to take your understanding to a deeper level or maybe have a reference that will jog your memory of a distinction, or a place to dig into a distinction, a bit deeper. This book is for you.

3) You are a beginning through established coach in a coaching discipline that does not reference the body. But you are curious about it as you have heard it referenced, or stumbled upon the body, or somatics, in your learning. You are curious to learn more about the body. This book is for you.

4) You are anyone else: a leader, an athlete, a psychologist, a social worker—i.e., someone interested in human performance and leadership. Or, perhaps, you are an acquaintance of the author, curious as to what the heck he actually does. This book may or may not be the book for you. If, however, you are intrigued as to what I have said so far, please keep reading.

As the subtitle of this book—*A Somatic and Embodiment Primer for Coaching In, With, and Through the Body for Coaches and Leaders*—states, this book is a *primer*.

Merriam-Webster dictionary defines a primer as "a small introductory book on a subject." That is exactly what this book is intended to be. It is not written to be *the* definitive book on coaching in, with, and through the body, but rather a place to start. It is written in an easy, fun manner with lots of illustrations to help coaches start or continue their journey of learning to coach in, with, and through the body. Many parts of the book are simplified, and an attempt has been made to boil down key ideas to usable, and easy to understand, concepts and ideas. If a subject or idea sparks in you a desire to dive deeper, reference sources are provided. Another key point around this idea is for the reader to allow the space for learning to be a starting point—it is not intended to be Truth with a capital T. It is the author's hope that this book opens a new domain of learning for the reader, not the final destination.

Just prior to jumping into the book we will have a quick discussion on the foundational assumptions of coaching in, with and through the body. The book is then written in three main sections. They cover the *Why*, the *Where/What,* and the *How* of coaching in, with, and through the body. We will then cover them in the following way.

≫ Section 1: The Why of Coaching In, With, and Through the Body

Why do we coach, in what one master certified coach has termed the "Holy Grail of leadership," the body? This section explores this question. It starts specifically with a definition of somatics. Once the distinctions are clear, we take a deep—and yet at the same time, if possible, light—dive into the biology of the human body and how our biological makeup creates the opportunity to coach in, with, and through the body. A portion of the reading will be greatly influenced by the research of Dr. Stanley Keleman and his foundational work on how the human body operates to create the humans we are and the emotions we experience. From there the book will explore the concept of somatic shape, how our shape is created, and how it influences how the world shows up for us. We will then explore how our body shape creates moods and emotions. This section wraps up with the exploration of practices and how they create and sustain our somatic shape. We spend a bit of time exploring trauma from a coaching prospective. From ontological coaching the book explores two key models in the discourse: the Observer, Action, Results (OAR) Model, and the Body, Emotions, and Language (BEL) Model. Additionally, I add a few bits of information to the BEL Model to further the learning, creating the Know Thy SELPH Model.

» Section 2: The Where/What of Coaching In, With, and Through the Body

The second section will look at this idea: when we say "coaching in, with, and through the body," *where* and *what* parts of the body do we actually coach in, with, and through? This section takes a deeper dive into established methodologies that explore the specific parts of the body we're referencing when we coach in, with, and through the body. Information on the methodologies, such as their histories, key researchers, and other attributes will be shared.

Among other distinctions, this section will cover topics such as:

• Chakras

• Body Armoring

• Archetypes and Bodies

• The Four Basic Body Shapes

• Look to the Hands

• The Fifth Body Shape: Center and Centeredness

• The Eight Basic Moods

• The Four Pivot Points

Additionally, there are accompanying illustrations to give the reader clues to possible routes and new awarenesses in and of the body.

» Section 3: The How of Coaching In, With, and Through the Body

The final section explores a question many coaches have: *how* do you actually coach in, with, and through the body? This section dives deep into some actual coaching moves and techniques to help coaches with a foundation for their own learning, and simplified step-by-step processes. First, though, the section establishes some foundational distinctions when coaching in, with, and through the body. The reader then explores the first of two bodies in the coaching conversation: their own body and how they might show up in the coaching conversations, and then is given practices to shift to a different coaching body. The second body explored will be the body of the coachee. To set up the coaching techniques, a brief look at the somatic arc of coaching will be explored to help the reader apply when to use the techniques.

There will then be a deep dive into several foundational somatic coaching techniques and possible tweaks of the moves to help coaches. The somatic coaching techniques explored are:

- Breathing, the fundamental somatic practice
- Centering Techniques
- The Scanner Technique
- Somatic Role Playing (SRP)
- Coaching to the Four (Plus One) Shapes
- Breath to Blend (BTB)
- Expand/Contract
- Coaching to the Speech Acts
- Coaching to the Four Pivot Points
- Coaching to Chakras/Body Armoring

The section then wraps up with some brief explorations of disciplines and practices to help the coach and coachee in the exploration of their bodies.

It is my hope that by the end of this book the reader will be much more equipped to understand the *Why*, the *Where/What,* and the *How* of coaching in, with, and through the body.

Foundational Assumptions

Before we begin our journey of coaching in, with, and through the body, it is critical to ground the core ideas on which this book is based. Here are some fundamentals.

- **Coaching in, with, and through the body is a skill,** like any other skill (woodworking, golf, knitting, or computer programing, as examples) that can be learned.

- Mastery of any skill is comprised of **knowledge (distinctions), understanding (language), motivation (emotions), and embodiment (body)**. Thus, to develop mastery in any skill, you must have knowledge of the skill, an understanding of how to do it, motivation to learn it, and, to bring it all together, you must embody the skill.

- The only way to **embody anything is to practice:** the more practice, the more something becomes second nature; i.e., it becomes embodied. Therefore, one must practice coaching in, with, or through the body. This cannot be learned in a simple course, by reading a book (even this one), and, most of all, it cannot be learned without repetitive practice.

These things cannot be circumvented. What we are good at, we have practiced, and to grow with something, we must continue to practice.

Therefore, let's begin—or continue—our practice of coaching in, with, and through the body!

Wait! This sounds like oversimplification! Is it? It depends . . .

As we start down this path of learning about coaching in, with, and through the body, we will be taking a subject which can fill many lifetimes of learning and putting it into a book of only a couple of hundred pages (a number of which are pictures). Some may say we are oversimplifying a very complex and deep subject with what you will explore in these pages. To that I say yes—in many instances we are taking something complex and making it simple. We do this because this is how we humans learn.

Take something that we can all do (since you are reading this): something simple like reading. Every one of you who is reading this book, at some point, did not know how to read. You could not understand simple written words such as *dog* or *cat*; you could not even make out letters. You started through learning simple things such as letters and sounds, working up to simple words like dog and cat. It was through the learning of the distinctions of letters and words that you would, at some point, string those words into sentences and then paragraphs—and so your learning began. And, at some point, you could read. But wait, there's more. Take the word *read*. It also can be pronounced "red"—as in, I read the book you gave me. Same word, differing meanings. (The second use is actually a past tense use—the action happened in the past—but still, the meaning is different.) You could not have the second, more advanced understanding of the word read without the first understanding. You had to start where you started.

We will be exploring coaching in, with, and through the body in the same way. There might be several ways to explore the body, and we might even find experts who claim that some of the distinctions in this book are incorrect. My goal is not to make this the bible of coaching in, with, and through the body, but rather to make it a place to start. As a result of reading this, you will not have a one-size-fits-all technology; instead you will have the beginnings of your learning of the body. Things you learn here will help establish a foundation for your learning about the body, and they are a place to start. If you are thinking that a distinction you learn here will be correct 100 percent of the time, I want to challenge your thinking. If, however, the learning here helps you to take your coaching deeper, if it helps your coachees (those you are coaching) gain the insights they are seeking in the coaching relationship, then this book has accomplished its goals. We start by learning distinctions, which are not "Truth with a capital T," but rather places to start. You will be learning distinctions which will help you coach in, with, and through the body.

At some point after you have started to wrestle with the distinctions in this book, those wrestlings might lead you to pick up another book on the subject. (And good news, there are lots of recommended readings in this book for you to further your learning.) Or perhaps you will want to take somatic coaching courses to develop your skills. It is from these additional readings and learnings that, hopefully, you will continue the road to mastery. It is when you are well down the road to mastery that the things you learn in this book may start to shift from over-simplification to, well, "it depends." If that happens, congratulations! You are farther down the path to mastery, and you just might be better able to coach in, with, and through the body.

Art + Science + Practice = Mastery

This book is about the *science*, so to speak, and lays the foundations of where to practice. The *practice* leads to the *mastery* and the *art*. This book is written to raise more questions than it answers. If that happens, it has served its purpose.

» PART 1

THE WHY OF COACHING IN, WITH, AND THROUGH THE BODY

The Why of Coaching In, With, and Through the Body

As we begin our journey into coaching in, with, and through the body, we start with the fundamental question of *why* we coach in, with, and through the body. To do this, we begin by defining the words *somatics, embodiment,* and *body*. With a working definition of *somatics* in place, we then shift the majority of this part of the book into the biological foundations of why coaching in, with, and through the body works, and the relevance of biology to understand this. This is followed with a chapter to explore why the idea of a "liquid accordion" is an apt metaphor for the body. We then will step through a brief exploration of moods and emotions and the body—and how the first two are created by the body as we navigate our world.

The section then changes directions a bit as we spend a chapter exploring trauma and its relevance to coaching in, with, and through the body. Part 1 closes with two chapters on the foundational methodologies of ontological coaching and the distinction of "Knowing Thy SELPH," a generative definition of how to frame the concept of the observer that makes each of us a unique "liquid accordion."

ONE

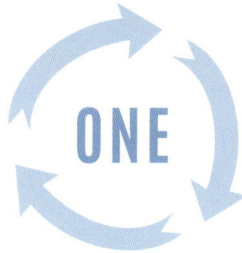

What Is Somatics?

Let's start at the very beginning
A very good place to start
From "Do Re Mi"[1]

As you are reading this book you will come across words like *somatics*, embodiment, and body in the context of coaching. The subtitle of this book—*A Somatic and Embodiment Primer for Coaching In, With, and Through the Body for Coaches and Leaders*—contains all of the three words. What are we attempting to say when we use these words? Throughout this book we will use these three—*somatic, embodiment,* and *body*—and their derivatives interchangeably. Here are some ways to look at what we mean.

Somatics

In his book *The Art of Somatic Coaching*, Richard Strozzi-Heckler writes: "The term *somatics* derives from the Greek *somatikos*, which signifies the living, aware, bodily person. It posits that neither mind nor body is separate from the other: both being part of a living process called the soma." In a conversation for the preparation of this book, Strozzi-Heckler further defined it as "the shape of our body in its livingness."[2]

Now for some dictionary definitions:

Dictionary.com defines somatic as "of the body; bodily; physical."[3]

Merriam-Webster on somatic: "of, relating to, or affecting the body especially as distinguished from the germplasm."[4]

Cambridge Dictionary defines somatics as "relating to the body as opposed to the mind."[5]

Embodiment

The late Wendy Palmer, a leadership embodiment coach and author of the book *Leadership Embodiment,* defined embodiment as "the living body in its wholeness."

Dictionary.com defines embody as: "to give a concrete form to; express, personify, or exemplify in concrete form."[6]

Merriam-Webster.com has embody as: "to give a body to (a spirit), to cause to become a body, to represent in human or animal form."[7]

Body

The word *body*, which almost everyone is familiar with, also has clear definitions.

Dictionary.com defines body: "the physical structure and material substance of an animal or plant."[8]

Merriam-Webster.com has *embody* as: "the organized physical substance of an animal or plant either living or dead."[9]

Cambridge Dictionary: "the whole physical structure that forms a person or an animal."[10]

For the sake of this book we include all of the above and define the subject *somatics / embodiment / body* as:

The living human body in its physicality, shape, and presence as it relates to how an individual perceives, senses, navigates, understands, and interacts with the world around themselves.

Coaching the Liquid Accordion

Coachee #1: Norman

Coaching in, with, and through the body can show up differently for many people. Here is one example.

Norman is a 45-year-old senior engineer in a mining company.

Norman lived in his head. He would show up at meetings and sit silently. However, he was not disengaged, as many thought, but rather quite engaged—in deep thought, listening for data and information that could inform his engineering decisions. Norman was a man who showed up as a brain on a stick, for all intents and purposes, someone who was disconnected from his body. He came to coaching at the request of his manager, who believed Norman could bring much more to the organization as a leader of the company's engineering team. The manager's concern, and the concern of others, was Norman's lack of emotional awareness and emotional intelligence. This lack of emotional versatility was hindering him with his highly energetic and much more emotionally aware team.

Initially in his coaching sessions, Norman would get deep in his head and go into a long, methodical explanation of how he was seeing the world. His coach—understanding coaching in, with, and through the body, when opportunities presented themselves—helped Norman access his body.

That understanding, before, was non-extant to Norman.

How did he do this? How did Norman access his body through coaching? Hold onto that question. We will return to Norman later in the book.

* * * * *

Since we now have a working definition of somatics, let's go learn about it—and what a better place to start than with the building blocks of the body.

The Body in Language

Have you ever noticed how much of the English language uses the body to create clarity in understanding? Here are some popular idioms.

We sometimes need:
- a heads up
- to have our feet on the ground
- to stand on our own two feet
- to stand our ground
- to get a foothold
- to sink our teeth into something

And we sometimes don't:
- have a leg to stand on
- need things which cost an arm and a leg

TWO

Expansion and Contraction

"The very fact that some 34 trillion cells can cooperate for decades, giving rise to a single human body instead of a chaotic war of selfish microbes, is amazing."[11]

Why do we coach in, with, and through the body? This is a question I believe I asked myself many times as I began my journey as a coach. I do remember early in my training as an ontological coach that coaching around the body seemed as foreign to me as rocket science, and not surprisingly, my awareness of my body was quite low at the same time. If you, the reader, have some similar perspectives, then let's get going on this. As this section unfolds, allow the space to not only permit you to learn intellectually, but also to start the process of learning in, with, and through your body. As different aspects of the body are explored, see if you can actually feel what we are discussing. Let's then learn about the why of coaching in, with, and through the body.

Biology 101: Cells in Action

Let's take a dive into the body and biology. Now, for our purposes, this will be a simple dive into these two things. As we explore concepts, don't worry about the exact biological processes or chemicals involved; we won't go that deep, but rather just seek

to grasp the main concepts. We start with a simple thing: a human cell. As the quote at the beginning of the chapter points out, we are made up of *a lot* of them, with estimates ranging from somewhere around 5 trillion to upwards of 70 trillion cells in an average human body. For our sake, we will start with just one cell.

Pick a cell, any cell—for our purposes, let's pick a simple tissue cell somewhere in the body. Remember, at this point we are just exploring the concept. So what is a cell? Fundamentally, it is a little drop of (mainly) water in various forms: gas, vapors, liquid, and other things like proteins and hormones. Around the outside of the cell is a membrane. Now this cell, like any other cell made of water, is not a set shape but rather takes a form that is always moving in all directions. A simple way to look at this is to think of a cell somewhat like a water balloon. (I told you this was going to be simple.) If you've ever held a water balloon, it is squishy and moves very easily. A term used for cells that are capable of movement is motility. The motility of cells is important as it helps the cell take on different shapes.

A *Liquid Accordion* Must Read

Emotional Anatomy by Stanley Keleman. If you find the idea of expansion and contraction interesting, a great place to look deep into the subject is Keleman's book. Now out of print, this 160-page deep dive of how moods and emotions are created in the body is a must read for coaches interested in the subject. Filled with numerous detailed drawings, the book is a foundational work on how to understand somatics and will open many possibilities to further explore the body.

So we have this cell, which lives in the real world along with trillions of other cells that partner with it to make up a human being. Now we add in simple physics. How is the environment of the cell affected by physics? First, there is pressure from inside the cell for the liquid to want to break free from the membrane. Think of a simple drop of water on a table; if you tilt the table, the water will move. There is also pressure from outside forces such as other cells, gravity, and motion—pressure for the liquid to be pushed back in on itself. If we were to push the water droplet into the table, and did not

allow space for the water to move, at some point we could not push the water into itself any more. This constant back-and-forth of pressures and gravity is at work on the cell.

This water balloon of a cell, then, is at all times trying to deal with the environment around it. Fortunately for the cell, because of its motility, it has a couple of options. It can expand or contract to deal with the ever-changing environment it finds itself in. As the location around the cell expands, the cell can expand to new space and to its physical limits. As the space and forces outside the cell contract, the cell can contract with it. Both the expansion and contraction take place to the limit of physics. The cell will expand to the limit that the cell membrane will allow, and it will contract to the limit that physics will allow. All of this is influenced by things like hormones, temperature, pressure, and more. We could go deeper into this, but the essential takeaway is that cells fundamentally . . .

Expand and Contract

They expand and contract to deal with the forces around them. This expansion and contraction is important to us, and we will see it again.

The *Liquid Accordion* in Action 《 《 《 《 《 《 《 《 《

It can take up to 200 muscles for a human to take one step. That is a lot of expansion and contraction of muscles, and just to move a single foot. Imagine how much expansion and contraction must happen to do something more complex like sprint, run a 10K, or dunk a basketball?

So what's next? At the next step in our exploration, cells join with other cells of the same type and begin to form layers. A simple example is the skin on our body. Skin is layers and layers of cells, and as the cells take on different compositions the layers themselves become different. Imagine the layers of skin cells, muscle cells, fat cells, etc. Now if we take a bunch of cells and they form a layer, at some point the layers form tubes. In your body, now, think of veins, capillaries, and, on a larger scale, bronchial tubes and the stomach. For our reference, think of a simple drinking straw. It is layers of cells of a certain type, and it allows what? The tubes allow some liquid to move from one location to another. In the case of our exploration, other cells—for instance, blood cells—allow water, plasma, hormones, nutrients, and more to move from place to place. How do these cellular tubes get the liquid from point A to point B? Guess what? These cellular tubes move liquids by . . . you guessed it . . .

Expansion and Contraction

When the tube expands, it creates a vacuum to attract the liquids to the space, or it can contract and force the liquids out of the tube. With either option, the tubes in their simple states expand and contract in unison to move liquids of some sort throughout the body. Think of your body at this very moment. Right now there are thousands of miles of tubes, such as veins and arteries, currently expanding and contracting, to send blood throughout your body. Ever been lightheaded? What happens when a person

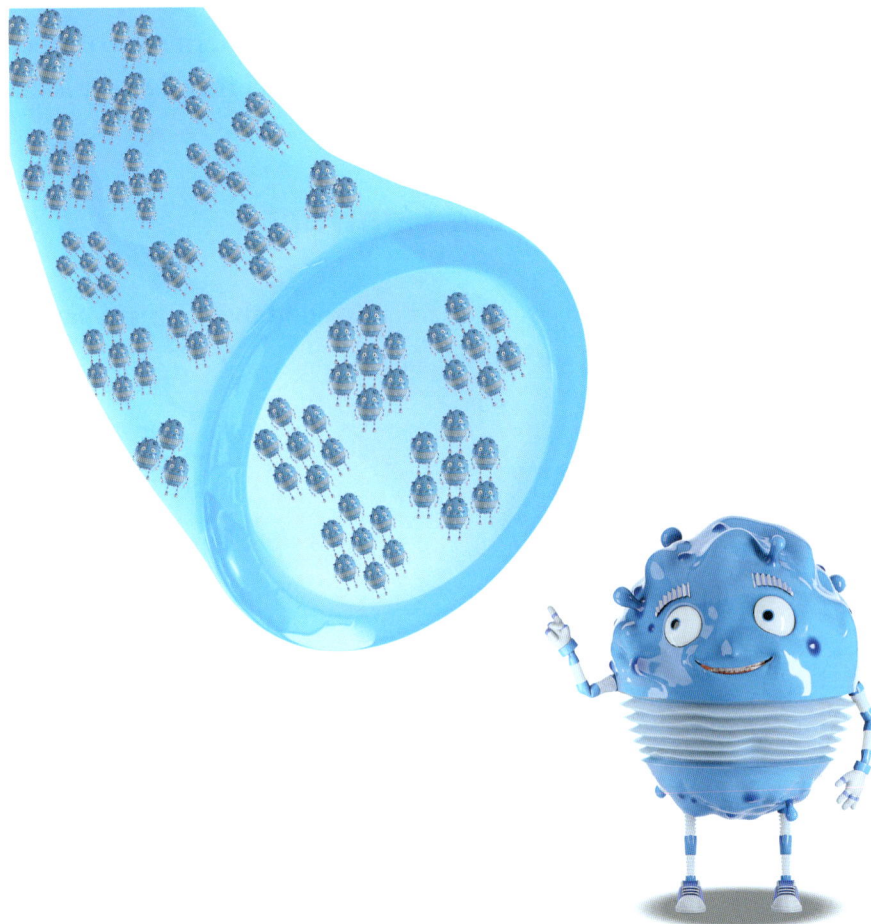

experiences this feeling? The blood vessels in a person's head are contracting, and blood and oxygen are not getting to the head region in normal amounts, and you feel, well, lightheaded. All of this is the trillions of cells expanding and contracting.

At some point these cells, layers, and tubes form organs. Fundamentally, what do organs do? They:

Expand and Contract

Two great examples of organs are the heart and lungs. The heart is fundamentally four chambers with layers of cells around them which then expand and contract to move liquid (blood infused with the gases O2 and CO2) throughout the body. The lungs are two chambers of small tubes which expand (bring air in) and contract (send air out), a process called respiration. Like the heart, the lungs at their simplest are vast amounts of cells, layers, and tubes that fundamentally expand and contract. What about muscles? They are basically tubes that either expand or contract. We could explore all organs in the body, but fundamentally, they are all some combination of cells, layers, and tubes which expand and contract to move some liquid, gas, or the like through them. One exception is the brain: it moves electrical currents—which is sort of the same—but not

The *Liquid Accordion* in Action « « « « « « « « «

It has been estimated that in an average person's life he or she will consume more than 12,000 gallons of water (greater than 45,000 liters, for our metric friends). That's a lot of H20 needed to keep the liquid accordion we call humans in action.

something we will dive into in this book. Another exception is bone, which for the most part is solid, but it is necessary at the anchor points for muscles to expand and contract. Without the skeleton the body could not take its shape—but more about shape later.

For simplicity, though, the takeaway from all of this is that, at the basic level—through cells, layers, tubes, and organs—we as humans fundamentally work through the physics of expansion and contraction. To recap, the takeaway is that, as humans, we are always . . .

Expanding and Contracting

THREE

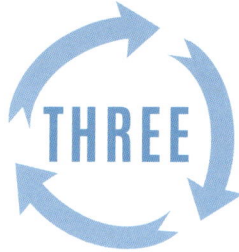

The Liquid Accordion

"At our core we are liquidity in partnership with its vessels and tubes."
Stanley Keleman[12]

Let's leap forward from this foundation that the body is made of cells, layers, tubes, and organs that are in never-ending states of expansion and contraction. If we take these trillions and trillions of cells that form layers, tubes, and organs and put them all together, we get the amazing thing called the human body. At any given time, the expansion and contraction of these trillions of cells create infinite possibilities for the human body to take action. The body can stand up, sit down, wave, walk, cry, jump, sleep, talk, tiptoe . . . and countless other options. To do this takes the coordination of all of these cells, layers, tubes, and organs in unison. A great way to look at this is to imagine the human body, made up mostly of water, as a huge liquid accordion (hence, the catchy title of this book). I know we have used the phrase earlier in the book, in the introductory material and in some sidebar elements, but let's officially introduce, or think of it, in this way now. Expanding here, contracting there, and then contracting here and expanding there, all in the span of seconds, into minutes, into hours, into days, into our lifetime as a human. This liquid accordion, then, is constantly in motion, and this motion is, at the cellular level, simple expansion and contraction.

Think of the trillions of cells that have to work in unison for a human body to do something as simple as stand up. Imagine yourself sitting in a chair. If you are actually sitting at this moment as you read this, you can even play along. As you are sitting there, what would you have to do to stand up? Assuming you have conscious thought to think to yourself, you will think something like: *I will now stand up.* What will happen, and where, in your body? If you are sitting in a chair with armrests, you will likely start by contracting your muscles in your hands to grab the handrest and contract your chest muscles and arm muscles to pull your body forward. Meanwhile, your muscles in your rear end might contract to facilitate the move forward. Your lungs might expand to take in a breath of air as you are rising, and to do that your abdominal muscles might expand to allow for an expanded midsection. All of this and more, in just a fraction of a second, perhaps, just to start the action of standing up. We could go on and on, and at some point, in a matter of a couple of seconds, your body will be standing erect, out of the chair. All with the basics of expanding and contracting, all done by this amazing liquid accordion.

If we were to have the ability to witness every person standing up from a chair we would likely see that there are some similar expansions and contractions in each person. We would see some contraction of certain muscles to stand up. We would also see, though, that each person may have a different order of how they expand and contract to stand up. You may tilt your head down and lead with your chest as you stand up. I may tilt my head up and lead with my jaw as I stand up. As much as we have similar expansions and contractions, we may also have different expansions and contractions. All of this is due to the literal shape of our bodies.

Shape and the Liquid Accordion

Each person, then—each liquid accordion—over time evolves into a literal shape. Imagine your world. Do you know people who are tall? People who are short? How about people who are thin, who are overweight? Take it deeper, though. Do you know people who seem to always be smiling? How about people who always seems to have

The *Liquid Accordion* in Action « « « « « « « «

Observing the Liquid Accordion in the Wild: People Watching

Want to have some fun the next time you're out in the real world? A great practice to observe the liquid accordion in its natural habitat is People Watching. Whether you are at the mall or in an airport, liquid accordion people watching can be a fun way to start to learn much about the body, not only by watching other people but also to see if you can, so to speak, embody them. Obviously, you will need to do this from afar. The goal is not to make others feel uncomfortable, but rather to attempt to see the world through their eyes and their body. Some examples:

· When walking in a place like an airport, from gate to gate, observe individuals in front of you also walking.

· Walk the way they are walking.

· Walk at the speed they are walking.

· Swing your arms the way they are swinging their arms.

· Hold your head the way they are holding their head.

· Try to imitate anything specific in their body movements.

As you are doing this, notice how the world looks to you in the moment. Does the world seem to slow down? Does it seem to pick up its pace? Does it seem smaller? larger? Whatever you notice, be curious about. What would the world look like if this was the way you habitually navigated the world? Remember, we see the world not as it is, but rather as we are.

a scowl on their face? People who seem to be leaning forward when they walk? People who walk fast, people who walk slow? Observe the people around you, and you will likely see bodies that, with a little observation, are quite unique in shape to each person. It is the literal unique shape that makes each of us that we will explore in detail.

The liquid accordion that is our body has a shape. For you it might be a thin, elongated body, whereas someone else has a rounder, more condensed body. You might have a face that is round, always smiling, while someone else might have a taut face, one that seems to be emotionless. When you sit, you might sit with an erect spine, almost formal, with a rigid and tense backbone; someone else might have a rounded, more informal way of sitting. We are talking here about the literal shape of the body. Each body is different, and each body is unique. It is the shape of the body that determines many things, and we will explore them in this book in detail. But first, a bit more on our shape.

First Humans

How are we as humans shaped? We start before birth. In fact, let's go back millions of years. Back to when humankind left the water and evolved into whenever we decide that humans became humans—fundamentally, when we as a species stood up. Standing up was a huge evolutionary leap for humankind as, by standing up, what we did was expose all of our vital organs—heart, lungs, kidneys, genitals (yes, even those), and much more—to the world. Humans are one of the only species to do this. This was not without risk, though, as to stand up meant that the harsh world we lived in was now exposed to organs necessary for our survival. Around the same time we were also developing a way to make assessments about our safety and survival, about our moods and emotions. These moods and emotions were (using a definition we will explore more later) a predisposition to action. They were also tied to our body as certain moods and emotions were tied to protecting the body (i.e., contracting) and others were tied to a perception of safety (i.e., expanding). This is a quite simplified version, for our sake, though expansion and contraction are integral to how we then navigate the world as modern humans.

Pre-Birth

We are historical beings. For each individual to come into this world we must have the genetic DNA and building blocks of our parents, grandparents, great-grandparents . . . all the way back to whenever we began. We also have their histories. Their trials, tribulations, the paths they took to our conception. For the moment, let's just explore you, the reader. Think about your parents. What part of the world did they come from? What race, what genetic makeup did they provide you with that makes you uniquely you?

How about your parents' history? Did they come from a background more physical in nature, i.e., more manual labor, or did they come from a more intellectual background, more thinking? Did your parents grow up in an environment where fresh, healthy foods were available? Maybe your parents did not eat in a healthy way. Speaking of health, did your parents have a family history of longevity, or did they have a family history of dying early? Did you have parents with debilitating diseases? Did your parents grow up in a safe existence, or did they grow up in a rough environment? Did your parents grown up in a world of excess and wealth? Middle class? Or a lower, less economically robust world?

We could go on and on. The point is that a very large number of variables came into play that led to the moment that you, as a human, were conceived, and all of those variables influenced the shape that you became before you were even conceived. All of those factors show up in the DNA that is uniquely you.

Conception to Birth

Your shape is greatly influenced by multiple factors from conception to birth. Things such as your mother's health during your gestation period. What was her stress level, her fitness level? Did she smoke cigarettes; did she drink alcohol? Did your mother have an easy pregnancy, or was it a difficult pregnancy? How about your actual birth: was it long and difficult, or quick and without a hitch? All of these factors influence the shape that you are.

Birth

The actual process of birth can have a profound effect on one's shape. The process of going through the birth canal, in itself, affects the shape of a baby's body. The actual process squishes and contorts the body. Overly traumatic births can have effects on how the baby enters the world, with all the pressure of the birth stressing the baby as it enters the world. Babies born through cesarean section are shaped by the birth in that they do not have severe pressures on their body in the profound moment of birth.

Early Childhood

Think of a newborn baby. Among the many words we could use to describe them: cute, soft, cuddly. But, for instance, we could also describe them as blobs. What I mean by that is when a baby is born its shape is present and yet not completely defined. The baby's body is elastic and flexible, allowing for the baby to make it out of the birth canal. It is in early childhood that a baby's shape starts to really form. Prior to birth it is our histories and genetics that shape us; after birth it is life that shapes us.

During early childhood our shape is greatly influenced by our caregivers and family. Again, let's have you look at yourself and your early life. Think back to your childhood. Did you grow up in a loving family? A family that gave lots of physical touch and tenderness? Was your primary caregiver your mother? father? grandparents? a nanny? Any combination of these? Were your caregivers loving? distant? cold? How your primary caregivers raised you allowed the space for your shape to start to take hold. For instance, if at an early age you were taught that your caregivers were loving and open, that affected your shape.

How about your family? Did you have many siblings? If you did, were they your age? Your gender? Did you and your siblings, if you had them, play together, or did you grow up in a more singular world? Was your play rough and tumble, or more timid? Things such as the size of your family, the ages and genders of those around you, all affected the shape you are now.

Communities

After the immediate family, we are also shaped by the communities we grew up in and lived in as members. Thinking back, did you live in a tight-knit community? Did you grow up in an urban setting or a more rural setting?

Some examples of communities:

- Neighborhoods

- Village/town/city

- State/regions

More questions to explore around communities:

- Was the community you grew up in inclusive or exclusive?

- Was the community racially/ethnically influenced?

- There are likely many more you can think of!

The *Liquid Accordion* in Action

More of the Body in Language

We can have:

- knee-jerk reactions

- a brain drain

- a gut feeling

- a gut reaction

- a stick up our ass

- a bug up our ass

- our back against a wall

- skeletons in our closet

- butterflies in our stomach

- our head in the clouds

- the weight of the world on our shoulders

- a sweet tooth

- something on the tip of our tongue

- two left feet

Institutions

We are shaped by institutions. Some examples:

- Schools

- Military

- Church/religious institutions

- Civic organizations

- Fraternal organizations such as scouting, fraternities/sororities, even gangs

- Organized physical activities/sports

Some questions to explore around institutions and how they shape us:

- Was the institution formal or informal?

- Did the institution in which you were involved attract you to it, or was it forced upon you?

- Were there strong norms in the institution, implied instructions as to how you were supposed to act and behave?

The *Liquid Accordion* in Action « « « « « « « « «

Fun Exercise

As we near closing this chapter, what is the shape of your liquid accordion? Start at the top of your head and "scan" though your body. Are you aware of where there is tension in your body? Are you aware of your shape? There is not a right or wrong with our shape; there can be, though, situationally effective and ineffective shapes that expand or limit our abilities to navigate the world around us.

The beauty of the study of somatic and ontological coaching, and this book, is it allows individuals to shift their shape, creating a shape that serves us as we navigate the world around us.

- Did the institution cater to a certain demographic such as race, gender, income, or social status?
- Did the institution have requirements and/or expected ongoing commitments?
- Were there punishments or repercussions for certain behaviors?

For instance, did you grow up in a city such as New York, in a tight-knit community, or did you grow up, perhaps, on a rural farm? Did you grow up in communities within your community?

Environment

Environment also plays a part in our shape. Growing up in a more natural, outdoor environment will shape us, but so will growing up in a densely packed urban setting.

We Have a Shape; We Also Have a Non-Shape

As humans, we have a shape. The shape of our body determines how we navigate the world around us. Just as we have a shape, we also have a non-shape; that is, whatever our shape is, it means we cannot be, at the same time, a different shape. For example, let's say that I have the shape of someone who is very resolute and a body that is hard and muscular. I navigate the world by force and control my feelings. At the same time, my non-shape means that I will usually not have an openness to feel a variety of emotions in the moment. To experience our non-shape will take practice and new learning as we navigate around many of our patterns that have created our shape. More on this later in the book.

Coaching the Liquid Accordion

Coachee #2: Rebecca

Unlike Norman, Rebecca was someone who lived in her body. Trained as a gymnast from the age of 3, she had channeled her love of music and dancing onto the mat with vigor and enthusiasm. Throughout her preteens, every waking minute seemed to be dancing, singing, and tumbling. But a broken leg when she was a teenager meant the end of her gymnastics career—though not her enthusiasm for being in her body. This led to an active life in sports and fitness, and by her early thirties she was an extremely competent yoga and Pilates instructor. She came to coaching at the suggestion of a mentor who Rebecca had relied on to help her navigate the strong emotions of a toxic manager who left her questioning her confidence and abilities as the leader of a marketing department. This had been a job—until the new manager over her, at least—she had loved.

When she showed up at her intake session with her coach, she revealed that she was struggling with her job because she found she could not leave its stresses at work. She was stressed at work, which meant she was stressed at home, and she did not know how to "leave work at work," nor how to navigate her "boss from hell." As her coach listened, he realized that much of what would serve her was her body. She was blind to the body at the moment, as she was so entrenched in what was going on in her head . . .

Hang on to this story. We will meet Rebecca again later in the book.

FOUR

The Liquid Accordion
and Moods and Emotions

"Do emotional experiences and psychological beliefs shape
body tissue and structure, or does the structure of the body predispose it
to specific emotions and attitudinal sets? The answer seems to be . . . both."
Ken Dychtwald[13]

Imagine I shared something absolutely shocking to you. It is so shocking it throws you for a loop. Now imagine that, unknown to you, I filmed you when I was sharing the shocking thought or idea with you. What do you assess we would see? Here is what I assess we would see.

It is likely that if we replayed and slowed the video down as I shared the shocking news, your head would pull back quickly, as would your chest and shoulders. Your eyes would open wide, scanning the environment, as your mouth opened and you inhaled a large, quick breath of air. The oxygen you inhale would be quickly sent through your body to your brain, which is currently in overdrive trying to make sense of the situation. Your body would be instantly producing adrenaline to jump-start your heart and get your body to take quick, decisive action: action of either flight, fight, or freeze as the brain works to process the data and determine the best course of action to deal with what it has learned.

My assessment is that you would agree with what we would see. The reason we can predict this is that an emotion such as shock is universal in humans. Whether you live in Singapore or an indigenous tribe deep in the Amazon River Basin, we all, as humans, experience the same somatic reactions to something like shock. We may have different meanings and definitions of what just happened, but our bodies will react in fundamentally the same way if we are experiencing something like shock. Emotional states in the human body are universal among humans.

Let's return to the idea of us being a liquid accordion. In an oversimplified way to look at this, the idea that we as coaches want to understand is that, as our bodies expand and contract, the expansion and contraction creates different hormones and neural patterns which create the many moods and emotions we experience. When our bodies are in a particular shape over a longer time, we define the emotional state as a *mood*. A mood, from a somatic perspective, is a shape that our body regularly experiences which creates the predisposition to action running in our backgrounds. Emotions, on the other hand, are created when our body quickly shifts to engage with an external factor such as a conversation or viewing an event. This rapid change in our body again creates hormones and neural patterns that help us navigate a situation. Emotions, then, from a somatic perspective, are a temporary shape that our body experiences in a relatively short period of time which helps us navigate ever-changing external situations such as news, conversations, interactions, or events.

As an example, let's use a hypothetical situation. Unknown to you, you are someone who lives in a mood of resignation. As you navigate the world on a daily basis, your mood shows up in your liquid accordion of a body as slumped shoulders, head and eyes generally down, and a sigh in your voice and in the disposition of your body. (We will explore more of this in Part 2 of this book.) One morning you are walking to work in this mood of resignation.

Mood of Resignation

As you head down the street, you encounter your old boss, who still works for your old company who fired you from your previous job. Seeing this former boss creates in you an emotion of anger, and this changes your shape from quiet resignation to one of acting against your boss.

Mood of Resignation   *Encounter Old Boss*   *Emotion of Anger*

After your episode with your old boss—where, perhaps, you got to tell him what you thought about him, really letting him have it—you start walking down the street, a bit elated at your victory, and look down to see . . . a hundred-dollar bill on the ground. As you bend over, you look around and see no one else around possibly searching for this lost money, and you put the bill in your pocket. You are really in an emotion of elation now.

Emotion of Anger   *Find $100*   *Emotion of Elation*

As you think about what you can do with this one hundred bucks now burning a hole in your pocket, your mind wanders to either the new toy you can purchase for your hobby or the thought of treating your significant other to a great date night. In the liquid accordion of your body, life is now good! Not only did you get to yell at your old boss and "get even" with him, but you also just found one hundred dollars! As you're deep in thought, you hear your alarm on your watch beep telling you it's 8 o'clock, and you are now officially late to work, and you still have five minutes until you reach the office! Your emotion now shifts to one of being overwhelmed thinking about all you must do and what your boss will say about your tardiness. You enter an emotional state of being overwhelmed.

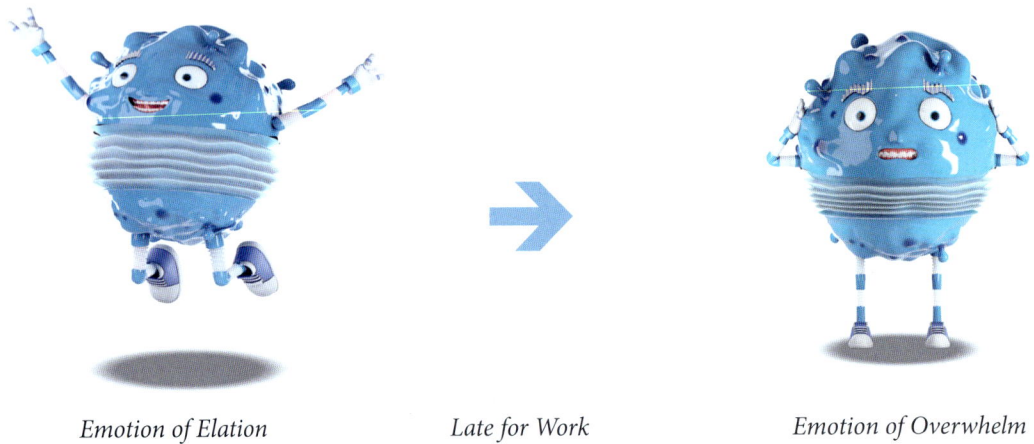

| *Emotion of Elation* | *Late for Work* | *Emotion of Overwhelm* |

As your emotion of being overwhelmed hits you, it causes your body to take rapid action to get to work before your boss finds out. You hurriedly slip in the back door of the office and move to your desk, quickly sliding into your seat. A few minutes later your boss walks by, seemingly unaware of your tardiness and, as you breathe a sigh of relief, your body contracts back to your underlying mood of resignation, a shape you know well, as you start to undertake the monotonous tasks of your job, a work position you hate . . .

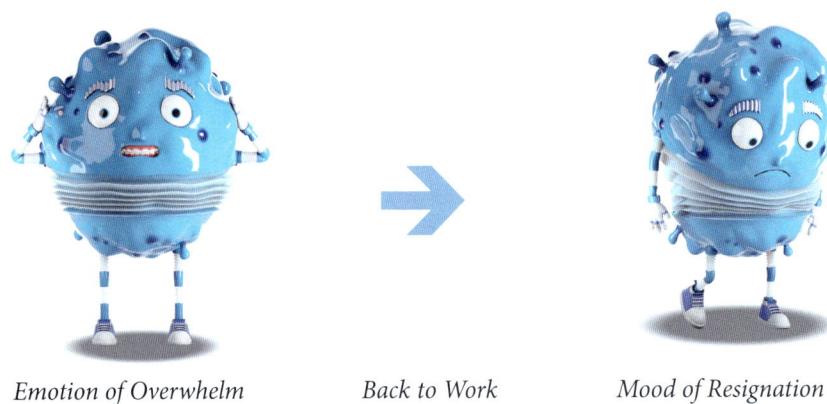

| *Emotion of Overwhelm* | *Back to Work* | *Mood of Resignation* |

That is, until something else happens and your liquid accordion expands or contracts to leave a new emotional state to deal with what happens next . . .

This liquid accordion goes through this expansion and contraction on a second-by-second, minute-by-minute, hour-by-hour, and day-by-day roller coaster as we navigate life. Not only does this happen for you, it happens to every person in the world, an ebb and flow of emotional states in our bodies, the liquid accordion alive and well, a place for coaching to make a difference.

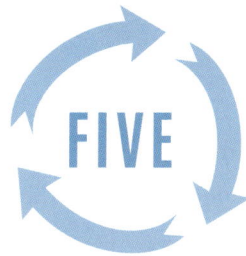

FIVE

The Embodied Pattern of the Liquid Accordion and Center

"My body is the shape I live in, and it shapes the way I live."
Raquel Welch[14]

As we explored in the last section, as human beings we are a liquid accordion navigating the world from event to event, conversation to conversation. Because we are historical beings (more about that later in the book), not every situation we encounter is new and unknown. Rather, it is quite the opposite; most of the situations we experience daily we have experienced in some form in our past history. The wisdom of our subconscious self is always running in the background, and the limbic system starts to notice patterns of situations and develops methods to deal with each of these events. To start, let's go back to being a baby.

When a baby is born the child is basically a big blob of tissue with all the biological matter that create the humans we are. There is some pre-programming in our DNA (the old nature piece), and as we grow and mature there is lots of learning (think the nurturing piece). The newborn baby, though, is completely reliant on its caregivers for every aspect of its survival: food, water, warmth, comfort, elimination of waste (they can't clean that dirty diaper themselves). Fortunately, the baby has an intense desire to learn to navigate the world. They do not do it themselves, though. They learn by watching others, most-ly—at least initially—their primary caregivers. Research has shown that when a baby experiences a new sensation such as a loud noise they have not experienced before, they will look to their caregiver, especially the caregiver's face. If, for instance, the baby sees in its caregiver's face a smile right after they hear the loud noise, they mimic and/or learn from the caregiver's body that this sound is not a threat. Babies fundamentally learn from those around them how to react to the world and its stimuli.

This does not stop as a baby grows, but as the infant grows the limbic system, as it matures, starts to recognize patterns and act accordingly. Thus, our shapes evolve over time and our embodied patterns become strengthened and more relied upon to deal with the situations we encounter as we navigate our world.

→	→	→	→
Event/Situation (Trigger)	**Somatic/Emotional Response**	**Event/Situation Managed**	**Shape/Observer Created/Reinforced**

As an example, let's say you are a leader who, when you are in your embodied pattern, raises your voice and uses forcefulness when you have someone who does not complete a task on time. As a result of raising your voice and using forcefulness, you have team members who work late to get things done on time. It might look something like this:

→	→	→	→
Employee Late With Project (Trigger)	**Boss Raises Voice And Forcefulness**	**Employees Work Late To Meet Deadline**	**Shape/Observer Created/Reinforced**

The takeaway is that we all have our embodied patterns, and they show up when they show up and how they show up. This is the liquid accordion in action. Like the adage, "If you only have a hammer, everything becomes a nail," this awareness of our embodied patterns allows us to develop better tools to manage the challenges we face. Instead of bludgeoning everything since we are a hammer, we develop a somatic tool-box that allows us to show up in a manner that better serves us.

Observing the Liquid Accordion in the Wild: People Watching (Part II)

Another way to observe others in their body is when you are sitting someplace like a crowded store watching people walk by. As you observe others, see if:

- you can gain some idea how this person "sees" the world based on the shape of their body.

More questions to ask:

- What clues can you gain that align with the embodiment patterns you see?
- What pace do you assess the person is walking at?
- Do you assess the person is present "in the moment," or do you believe they are moving more in their past or their future?
- Does the person seem connected to others, or disconnected?
- Does the person seem to have a light walk or a heavy walk?

Treat this practice as a coaching practice; the more you do it, the more you have access to clues as to how to coach someone. If, for instance, they are moving at a fast pace, how would you coach that person?

Have fun with this. The great part is this is a practice you can do, likely, every day.

As a coach, if we understand this, we can help the coachee begin to become aware of their liquid accordion and, when it is not serving them, we can help the coachee (through coaching) develop more effective and supportive ways of dealing with the challenges we face in life. What we are doing then is to help the coachee to *choose* their somatic/emotional response so that they can create/reinforce a *new* shape/observer.

When we as humans learn how to manage and shift our embodied patterns, we can influence how situations unfold by our choices rather than our embodied patterns. The model now looks like this:

→　　　　→　　　　→　　　　→

Event/Situation (Trigger)　　**Choose Our Somatic/Emotional Response**　　**Event/Situation Managed**　　**New Shape/Observer Created/Reinforced**

Just because we all have this *potential* to change our shape/observer, it does not mean we all have the *ability* to actually do so. This is where coaching and the ontological/somatic coach can help individuals shift their shape/observer and, as a result, shift how they see the world.

SIX

A Word About Trauma

"Traumatized people chronically feel unsafe inside their bodies: the past is alive in the form of gnawing interior discomfort. Their bodies are constantly bombarded by visceral warning signs, and, in an attempt to control these processes, they often become expert at ignoring their gut feelings and in numbing awareness of what is played out inside. They learn to hide from their selves."
Bessel A. van der Kolk[15]

Before we continue our exploration of the liquid accordion, I feel it is important to take a bit of time to talk about trauma and its relation to coaching in, with, and through the body. Various definitions of trauma abound, and for our purposes we will look to experts for their definitions.

The American Psychological Association (APA) defines trauma as "an emotional response to a terrible event like an accident, rape, or natural disaster. Immediately after the event, shock and denial are typical. Longer term reactions include unpredictable emotions, flashbacks, strained relationships, and even physical symptoms like headaches or nausea. While these feelings are normal, some people have difficulty moving on with their lives."[16]

Psychology Today, on its website, posted: "Trauma is a person's emotional response to a distressing experience. Few people can go through life without encountering some kind of trauma. Unlike ordinary hardships, traumatic events tend to be sudden and unpredictable, involve serious threat to life—like bodily injury or death—and feel beyond a person's control. Most important, events are traumatic to the degree that they undermine a person's sense of safety in the world and create a sense that catastrophe could strike at any time. Parental loss in childhood, auto accidents, physical violence, sexual assault, military combat experience, [and] the unexpected loss of a loved one are commonly traumatic events."[17]

Coaching, and coaching in, with, and through the body, is not therapy, and the two should not overlap. However, they may be close neighbors. The challenge for coaches—and therapists, for that matter—is where the line exists between whether a person has trauma or they simply have a somatic shape that was influenced by a significant event. From a coaching perspective, the International Coaching Federation (ICF) is not entirely clear on the distinction between where trauma ends and the "normal" events of life begin. The ICF even has certified some courses as Trauma Informed Coach training, further blurring the line.

Combine this with the challenge that even though coaching—and from our perspective, somatic coaching—is not therapy, the methodologies coaches use can have therapeutic qualities. Therefore, for the purposes for this book, we make the assessment that using these techniques to treat traumatic experiences for coaches is not recommended, as it is not the domain of coaching.

As a coach, should you encounter coachees with trauma-related issues, it is incumbent on you, the coach, to clarify with the coachee that coaching is not therapy, and you should refer the coachee to a qualified and licensed professional trained to deal with trauma. Our intent in this book is to use the information gained here only in coaching sessions and for the professional development of the coach.

SEVEN

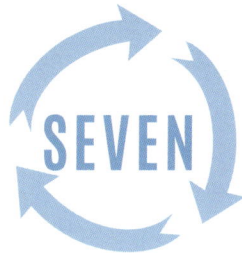

Ontological Coaching and Somatic Coaching as Methodologies

*"Stress is just that people do not know how to manage your body,
how to manage your mind, how to manage your emotions . . . "*
Sadhguru[18]

As we have established the biology of why we coach in, with, and through the body, we want to wrap it up with a methodology to frame our next section of the book: the *where* and *what* of coaching in, with, and through the body.

The practice of ontological coaching was developed by many founders in the field of coaching. Ontology is the study of what it means to be human, and this is the basis of ontological coaching. For our purposes we will briefly examine the foundations of ontological coaching as developed by the Newfield Network and, specifically, its founder, Julio Olalla. Olalla developed Newfield to be a "new field" of coaching, and two key models will further explain the methodology. As we unfold things in this book, these two models take the idea of the liquid accordion and explore the why of coaching in, with, and through the body.

O-A-R

We start with the idea that, as human beings, we take Actions (A) which lead to Results (R). This is the basis for what is called incremental learning. In incremental learning, if we want different results, the idea is that we take different actions to get different results. From a coaching standpoint, when we are coaching in this manner, we are in what is called transactional coaching; i.e., helping the coachee do more, or less, of the actions to get the desired result.

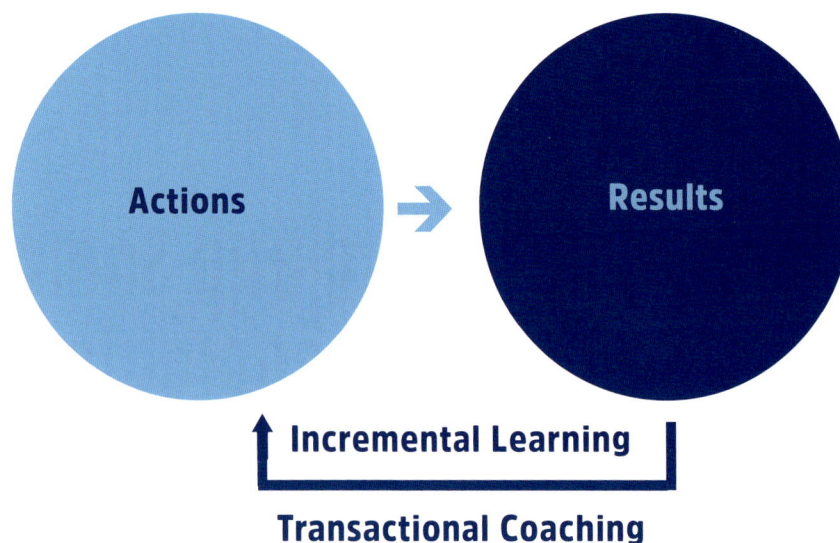

Incremental Learning

Transactional Coaching

Transactional coaching can be effective, and it works—until it does not. If it were this simple, all we would have to do as humans is read a book, and we would have perfect six-pack abs, perfect relationships, millions in the bank, and be completely happy. The challenge with transactional coaching is that when it does not work there is not much recourse but to keep trying different things to get different results. What is missing, though, is the O in the O-A-R model, and the O stands for Observer. The idea is that if I change the Observer of the situation, the new observer will see new and more powerful Actions to take to get new and more powerful Results. We call this Leap Learning, and it is the domain of transformational coaching or ontological coaching.

As an example, say you come to me and tell me you want to run a marathon in six months. From an incremental learning/transactional coaching perspective, I could say, "Great. Here is this great book on running a marathon, and all you must do is follow the directions. For instance, in week one you will run a total of 10 miles over three or four different days, and so on, until six months later you will run a marathon." There are people this has worked for, and it does serve a purpose in that, if you want to run the marathon, things are mapped out for how to do so. But what if you hate running, and the thought of even looking at buying a pair of running shoes puts a big pit of dread in your stomach? How likely are you to get up on Monday morning and lace up your

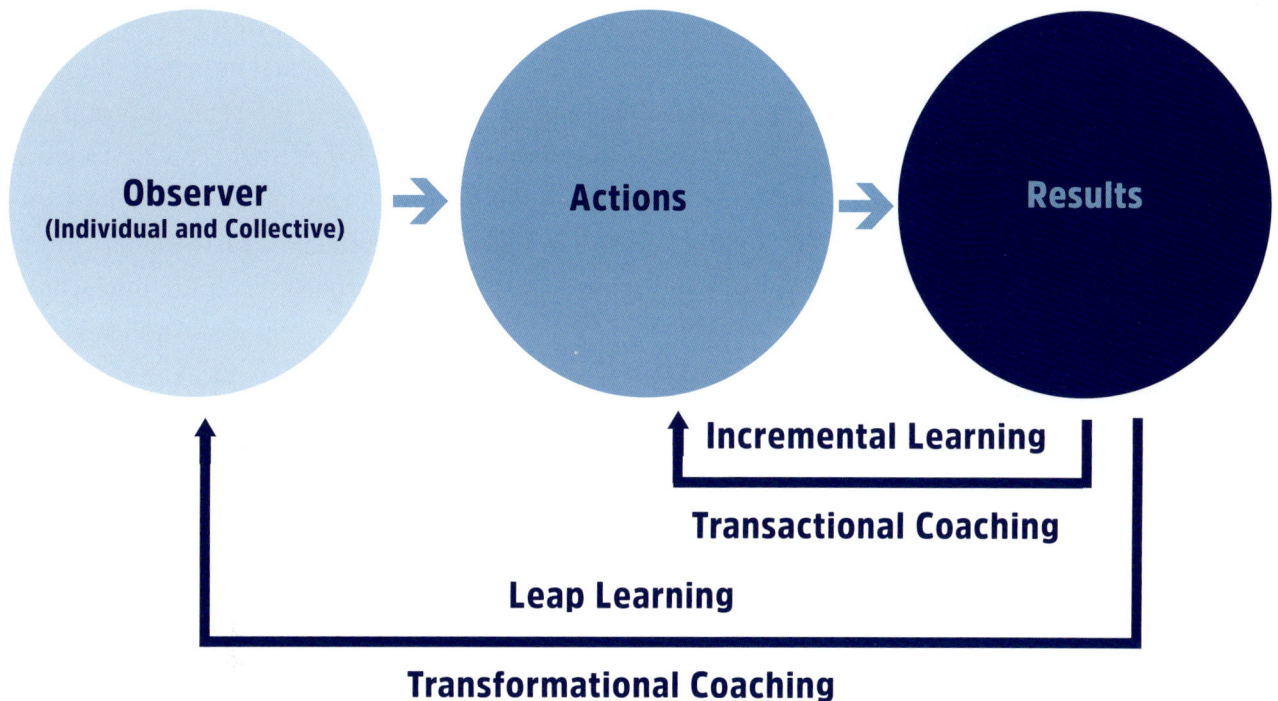

shoes and run three miles? My assessment is that you would not. Best-case scenario: you would begrudgingly run the first day but soon begin to find reasons to not run.

Conversely, have you ever met someone who absolutely loves to run? In fact, running is a key part of their life, and they do it six days a week, and they even share their day's run with you every day on social media. Key question: what if you could shift and see running the way they do? Chances are they see running as fun, purposeful, and a joyful experience. What if you could shift your observer to see running as *they* see running; what if you could experience running as fun and purposeful? If you could shift your observer to one that is conducive to running, you would, all of a sudden, see new and more powerful actions to take to create that new future. The question, then, is: how do we shift our observer? How do we create the possibility of leap learning? We have to look at what we call the B-E-L.

B-E-L

If ontology is the study of what it means to be human, what makes us human? Let us look at the B-E-L—but in reverse order—to unpack this.

L = Language

We start with the idea that we as humans live in language. Unless we are in deep sleep or a state of peaceful meditation, we spend our waking hours in language. We get up and immediately start an internal dialogue with ourselves about getting out of bed, going to

Language

the bathroom, brushing our teeth, and more, as we navigate our world. Language is the fundamental human technology. Think about a baby when it is born. It has one tool and one tool only, and that is the ability to cry. That cry at first sounds the same, but as the infant's caregivers we start to hear different cries: a hungry cry, a tired cry, a dirty diaper cry. As a baby grows, cries turn into sounds, sounds into words, words become sentences, and sentences in time develop into conversations. Conversations, both with ourselves and others, are how we navigate and make sense of the world.

On one hand language is descriptive, but it is more than that; it is also generative. Language does not just describe our world, it actually creates our world. How we see things—good, bad, fun, boring, and much more—all generate how we see the world. We also create and generate our future in language. Through language, we set up a meeting to be held tomorrow; we get married, through language; we create images through language. Think about the title of manager. There is not something that we can see and hold called a manager; it is a linguistic construction that creates, in our minds and in the minds of others, what that simple word means. We could go on and on, but for the sake of brevity, it comes down to this: we are linguistic beings.

»»»»»» The *Liquid Accordion* in Action

Still More of the Body in Language

Still more uses of the body in everyday language. We can be . . .

- lightheaded
- joined at the hip (with someone or something else)
- on our toes
- weak in the knees
- yellow-bellied
- heartbroken
- highbrow
- lowbrow
- browbeaten
- head over heels in love
- two-faced
- all ears
- on our toes
- head and shoulders above the crowd
- neck and neck with someone

E = Moods and Emotions

We are linguistic beings, and as human beings we are also emotional beings. To be human means we are always in an emotional state of being. We cannot *not* be in moods and emotions. And from an ontological coaching perspective, we define moods and emotions as a "predisposition to action." Specifically, we define moods as an overall way of seeing the world; they are the background lens through which we see the world. Emotions, on the other hand, are caused by events; they guide us into the actions we need to take to navigate the world. Think it through and this makes sense. As human beings we daily face large amounts of data constantly coming at us. As we wake and open our eyes, we start to collect data. We already have the background mood of how we are seeing the world. If we are pessimistic, we are (already) looking for the bad to come. Optimistic, and we are (already) looking for opportunities.

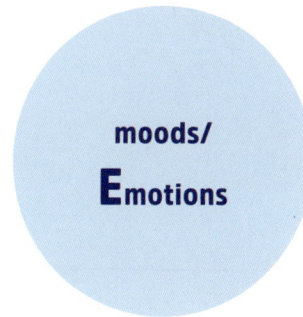

moods/ **E**motions

What time is it? What is the temperature in the room? Is there light coming in? As we get up and out of bed this data continues to accrue. We walk to the bathroom and have to navigate a dog sleeping in our path; yet, already, we are thinking about our day ahead. Data, data, and more data. But how to make sense of the data? That is where moods and emotions come into play. Moods and emotions are the filters that allow us, as humans, to determine which of the data is necessary to keep us safe, to take care of our cares. It is our moods and emotions which, as we said before, predispose us to certain actions. To have and be in moods and emotions is to be human, and we are always in some combination of moods and emotions, using them to navigate the world.

B = Body

We live in language, we have moods and emotions, and all of this resides in our body. We, as humans, are not just brains on a stick. Rather, as we have explored already in this book, we are in this amazingly complex and ever-changing liquid accordion that we call the body. The body is the domain of action; the body is where we interact with the world. Think about your brain. It is not a standalone entity but rather is part of a limbic system, residing . . . where? You guessed it:

Body

in the body. The body, through all our nerves, produces data which the brain then accumulates and uses to guide us to determine what actions we should take. Remember those things we just talked about: moods and emotions. Guess what? They reside in our bodies. In fact, how our body interacts with data (temperature, pressures, sensations, feelings, and much more) is transformed into moods/emotions which then determine actions we choose to take. For our purposes we will not go deeper into this in this section. (This is meant only as a baseline.) Rather, this entire book is about how to leverage this amazing thing called our body.

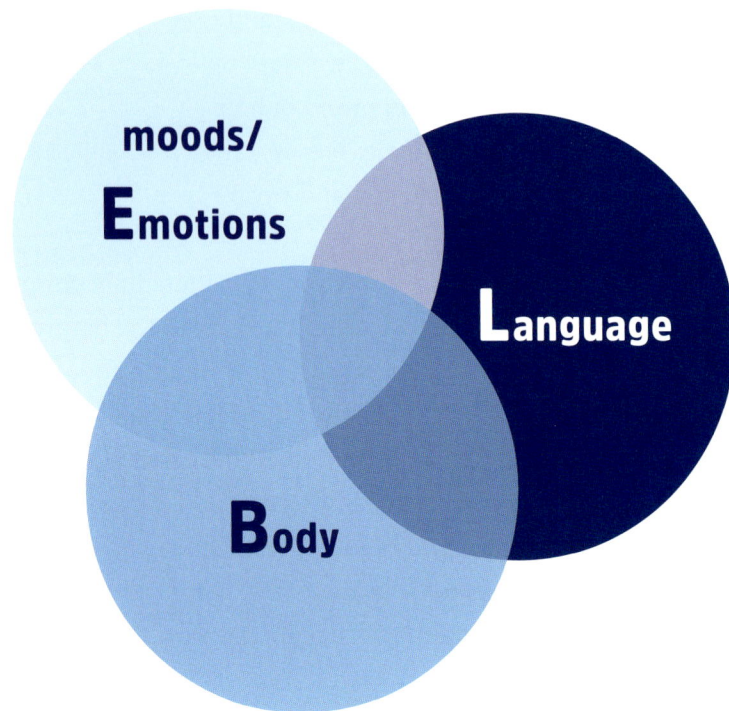

moods/
Emotions

Language

Body

EIGHT

Know Thy SELPH:
We Are Our Practices

"Anatomy is destiny."
Sigmund Freud

Know Thy SELPH

If we want to take the BEL just a bit deeper, we can add a few distinctions to bring it all together. We start with the BEL:

Body (somatics)
Moods/**E**motions
Language

We then add two more distinctions which also make us human:

We start with the idea that we are Historical beings. (I know it should be the next letter, perhaps, but it flows better to say "Know Thy SELPH" than to say "Know Thy SELHP"; work with me here. So let's cover this distinction at this point, but put it last in the acronym order.) We are our history. Think about all the history that led you to reading this book. As we discussed in the Liquid Accordion chapter, we are influenced all the way from our DNA to where we were when we were born, to caregivers, to our communities, institutions, and all of those seemingly random factors that create the unique shape we are. We cannot change our history, but we can become aware of how we were shaped by our history and how it affects how we see the world. Our history is where we get our context.

Historical discourses

We are also shaped by our Practices. As human beings we are always practicing, and what and how we practice we become good at. We practice our shape, we practice our emotions, we practice using language and the stories we tell ourselves. Over time we forget we are practicing all the things that make us ourselves. All these things determine what we see in the world. The great thing is, though, that if we want

Practices

to make changes in our life, we simply must change our practices. If we want to become more emotionally literate, we have to practice being in the emotions we want to feel. If we want to have better conversations, we must practice better conversations. If we want to have a body that serves us, we must practice it.

* * * * *

So, we want to strive to know thy . . .

Body (**S**omatics)

Moods/**E**motions

Language

Practices

Historical beings

And if we want to change ourselves, the good news is that we can change any of the above (the lone exception is our history; and yet, we can change how see our history). We can change our moods/emotions, we can change how we use language, and we can change our practices.

The B-E-L/SELPH and Congruency

A thought to bring it all together. When the BEL/SELPH is in congruency, we as humans are in a state where our body, emotions, and language (story) are all in alignment,

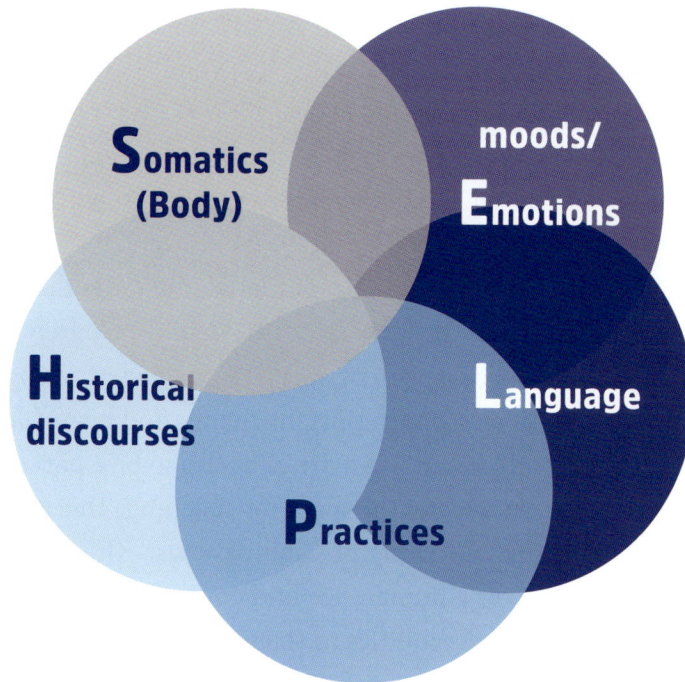

and we navigate the world in a manner that serves us and takes care of what we care about. It is when our body, our emotions, and our language are out of congruence that we find the possibility for coaching—specifically ontological and somatic coaching—to help the coachee find a way to take their observer to a place of congruence. Let's look at this in action.

Have you ever been in a situation where you had a gut feeling something is not right? For example, say your boss is in a powerful emotion of anger and you are the recipient of that anger. As your boss is "letting you have it," you stand there and take it. You are saying to yourself that what has transpired is not the truth, and you feel as though you should say something to your boss, but you cannot find your voice. But there is more: as you are thinking about saying something, your body is in a state of panic, and you feel your body shrinking and wanting to slink out the door and find a rock to hide under. Or, even better, perhaps, you want to plan your revenge and what you will yell back at your boss.

Yet, is this how you want to deal with your boss? If you could be out of your body, and be an observer of your observer, is this how you would want to act? I am guessing the answer is no. If you were you at your best, how would you handle this situation? If you could slow down time and really have a conversation with yourself and answer in a manner which is in alignment with your values, how would you respond? Would you be calm and relaxed, answering in a manner which, while listening to your boss, is ready to offer a different conversation with your boss, one that is able to handle the situation? Would you resolutely let your boss know that this is not how you want to have a conversation, and could you steer a new conversation into reality? All these options are available to you if you have the ability to shift your observer—and shifting to an observer that is congruent with who you are at your best.

An example of this in action is when someone has a so-called "wake-up call." It is the parent who ignores their health and body and lives unhealthily. Then that same parent has a child share with them, in a very emotional conversation, that they, the child, are upset and fear they will not have that parent at their wedding day because that person will be dead long before the child gets married. The parent, then, shifts their observer and makes their health a priority and now, instead of seeing exercise as hard, and definitely not fun, visualizes this important change and begins to make it to allow themselves to be a better parent and live a life of health to be a part of their child's life.

It is this incongruency that creates the space for coaching. This is where the ontological/somatic/transformational coaching possibilities exist. This is where we will go in the rest of this book. When, as a human, we find congruency in how we see, feel, and live in the world, we open up possibilities to shape our world and future. This is where coaching in, with, and through the body comes into play.

» PART 2

THE WHAT AND WHERE OF COACHING IN, WITH, AND THROUGH THE BODY

OVERVIEW OF PART 2:

. . . .

The What and Where of Coaching In, With, and Through the Body

Now that we have explored why we coach in, with, and through the body, we shift our exploration in this section of the book into the *what* and *where* of coaching in, with, and through the body. The purpose of this section is to help the reader have clarity on multiple methodologies and ideas as to where we coach in, with, and through the body and an understanding of the correlations of the body locations and various physical attributes and moods and emotions. To do this, we explore:

- The concept of the **chakras**, an ancient study of energy locations in the body and the understanding of both health and ailments associated with the chakras.

- The concept of **body armoring**, a methodology of exploring the idea of life energy being blocked in the body by armoring, limiting one's emotional growth.

- A large portion of this section is exploring the concepts of the four basic body shapes and how these body shapes manifest, fundamentally, in four ways of being; and then a fifth way of being: the concept of **center and centeredness**. An exploration of how these archetypes manifest in the body, along with common behaviors of each, is explored.

- An in-depth look at each of the **four (plus one) basic body shapes** is explored in a chapter for each. They are:

    - The Results Body Shape

    - The Spontaneous Body Shape

    - The Amiable Body Shape

    - The Methodical Body Shape

    - Center and Centeredness

- A "bonus" chapter on looking to the hands to further explore the four basic body shapes.

- A chapter on what is called the **8 Basic Moods of Life** is explored from the perspective of how moods/emotions show up in the body.

- The final chapter explores the concept of the **four pivot points** in the body. These are places where undue influence is placed in the body, and therefore are powerful coaching leverage points.

NINE

Chakras

"What happens when people open their hearts? They get better."
Haruki Murakami, Norwegian Wood[19]

The term *chakra* is from Sanskrit, means "disk" or "wheel," and is used to describe spinning energy locations throughout the body. Awareness of chakras has been around for more than 3,500 years, and it is likely known to individuals who practice yoga and other new age philosophies. In the domain of coaching in, with, and through the body, chakras can provide both the coach and coachee avenues for awareness and change.

Chakras describe these spinning points of energy in the body that regulate the life flow of individuals and therefore regulate how one interacts somatically with their world. The basic idea is that the life energy—or *chi* of an individual—flows throughout the body through the chakras. The more the life energy can flow through the chakras, the more healthily and vibrantly that individual will be able to navigate the world. There are different beliefs on the number of chakras, with up to 114 different chakras identified from different perspectives. Universally, though, there are seven major chakras identified, and each of the seven deal with one's life energy around aspects corresponding to each of the chakras. The chakras begin lower in the body and move upward, with each higher-level chakra opening up higher-level awareness and individual evolution. The seven major chakras are:

1) Root

2) Sacral

3) Solar Plexus

4) Heart

5) Throat

6) Brow

7) Crown

There are three fundamental states chakras can be in that determine and influence one's relationship with different aspects of their world.

- Deficient, or blocked: when a chakra is deficient or blocked we see limitations and challenges which stop the individual from effectively interacting with the world.

- Excessive: when an individual has a chakra that has excessive life energy flowing through it, the individual can experience "too much of a good thing" in that domain and, like deficiencies or blockage, this can lead to limitations and challenges regarding how the individual interacts with the world.

- Balanced: is when one's chakras are balanced and the amount of life energy is flowing through the body which allows the individual to more successfully navigate and interact with the world in his or her domains. Individuals who have balanced life energy flowing through their chakras show up in the world as healthy in all domains: physical, emotional, spiritual, and mental.

A very expansive body of knowledge exists in the study of chakras, and the goal here is not to teach the reader to become an expert on the chakras but to simply start an exploration of the topic. As each of the chakras is explored, we will briefly look at these designated topics:

Name: the chakra's Sanskrit name and literal meaning

Color: the chakra's color is how it relates to the frequency of the light spectrum of that chakra

Location in the Body: this is the physical location where you will find this chakra

Energy: this is the overall direction and intent of the energy

Element: the corresponding earth element that the chakra is associated with

How It Influences Us: these are areas in our lives where the chakra shows up and influences us

Physical Connections: the specific body parts and organs which are located and connected with the chakra

Qualities When Balanced: the healthy qualities we bring to the world when the chakra is in balance and alignment

When Blocked/Deficient: the unhealthy/limiting qualities we show the world when the chakra is blocked or deficient

When Excessive: the unhealthy/overused qualities we show the world when the chakra has excessive energy

Physical Ailments When Blocked, Deficient, or Excessive: common diseases and physical ailments that one experiences when the chakra is either deficient, blocked, or excessive

Each of the seven chakras are presented in chart/illustration form in the following pages:

Root Chakra

Name: *Muladhara* (root)

Color: red

Location In Body: bottom of the sacrum, base of spine

Energy: life force

Element: earth

How It Influences Us: basic human instincts, for survival: food, shelter, independence, groundedness, boundaries

Physical Connections: feet, legs, large intestine, sexual glands

Qualities When Balanced: survival, stability, grounding, prosperity, good health, vitality, well-being, comfortable in one's own body

When Blocked/Deficient: eating disorders, underweight, joint issues, knee problems, lack of focus, anxiety, disorganization

When Excessive: obesity, overweight, sluggish, tired, lazy, rigidity around boundaries

Physical Ailments When Blocked, Deficient, or Excessive: intestinal issues, issues with bones or teeth, issues with base of spine, legs, feet, knees, eating disorders

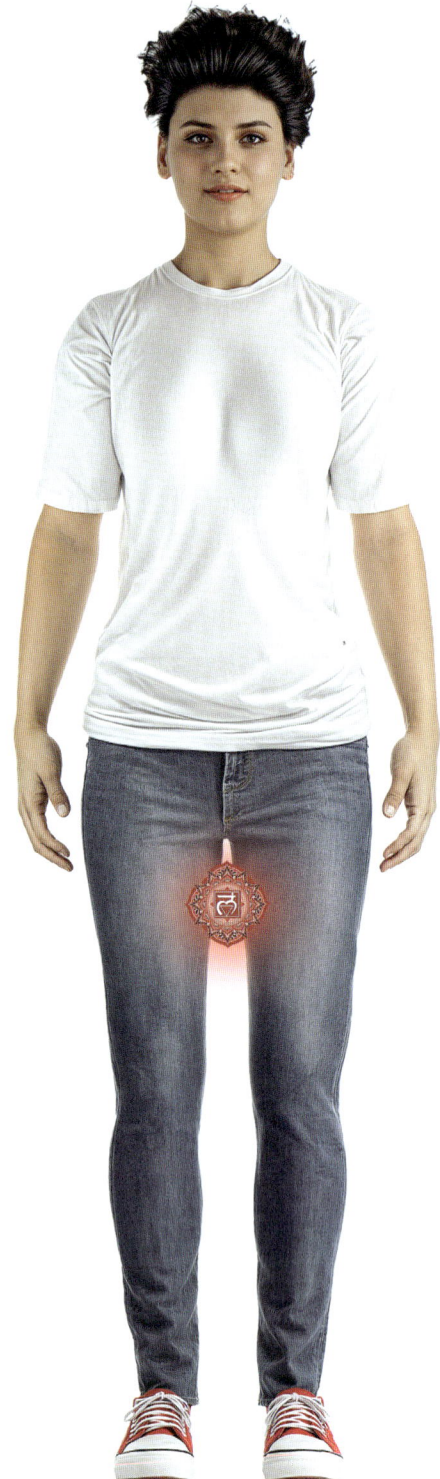

Sacral Chakra

Name: *Svadhisthana* ("your own place," "sweetness")

Color: orange

Location In Body: just below navel, parallel to sacral bone

Energy: emotions, desires, passions, sexuality, creativity

Element: water

How It Influences Us: sexuality, well-being, pleasure, emotions

Physical Connections: genitals, lower back, hips, lower internal organs (bowels, adrenal glands, ovaries, uterus, spleen, gall bladder, prostrate, kidneys)

Qualities When Balanced: emotional intelligence, healthy boundaries, graceful movements, healthy sexuality, healthy emotions, creativity

When Blocked/Deficient: frigidity and sexual issues, fear of change, lack of desire or passion, stoicism, denial of pleasure, lack of social skills, rigidity in one's observer

When Excessive: sexual excesses, addiction to pleasure, emotional roller coaster, emotional extremes (mood disorders, mania) obsessiveness

Physical Ailments When Blocked, Deficient, or Excessive: disorders with the reproductive system, sexual dysfunction, pain in lower back, knee troubles, lack of flexibility, numbed senses, menstrual issues in women

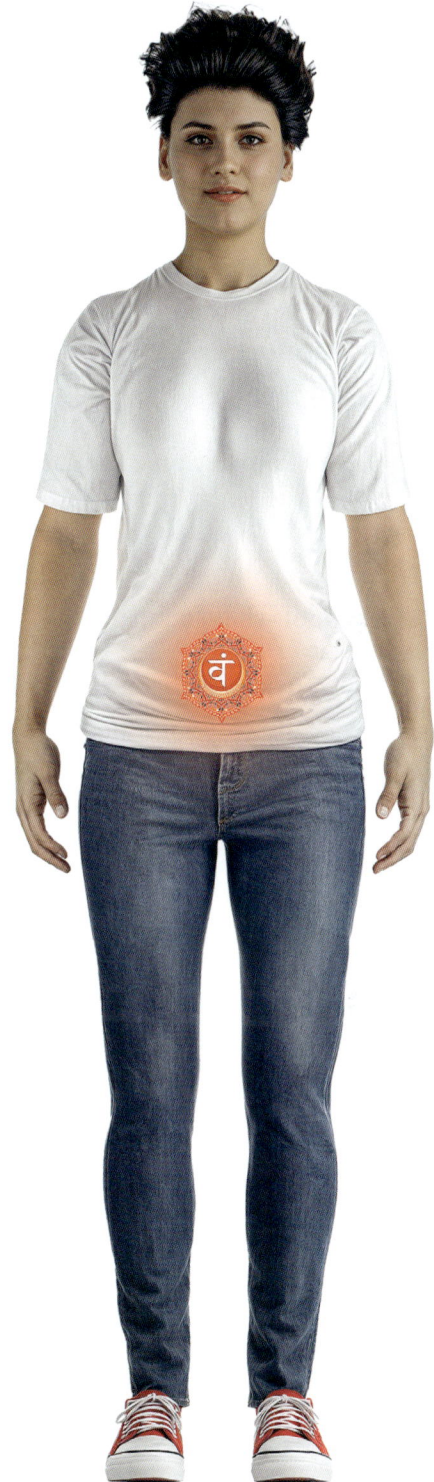

Solar Plexus Chakra

Name: *Manipura* (gem, lustrous gem)

Color: yellow

Location In Body: solar plexus (between the naval and below the sternum)

Energy: life force

Element: fire

How It Influences Us: self-esteem, confidence, will, power, activity

Physical Connections: stomach, pancreas, liver

Qualities When Balanced: self-discipline, responsible, personable, playful, spontaneity, sense of humor, strength of will and purpose

When Blocked/Deficient: timidity, lack of energy, chronic fatigue, poor follow-through, low self-esteem, emotionally cold, victim mentality, unreliable

When Excessive: control issues, never slowing down, anger issues, dominating personality, aggressive, need to be right, temper tantrums, ambition, arrogant, manipulative

Physical Ailments When Blocked, Deficient, or Excessive: digestive issues, ulcers, fatigue, hypertension, eating disorders, muscle disorders

Heart Chakra

Name: *Anahata* (unhurt or un-struck)

Color: green

Location In Body: heart area, center of chest

Energy: love and relationships

Element: air

How It Influences Us: love, happiness, inner peace, self-love, intimacy

Physical Connections: heart and lungs

Qualities When Balanced: loving (both of self and others), compassionate, empathetic, altruistic, peaceful, healthy immune system

When Blocked/Deficient: loneliness, depression, fear of relationships and intimacy, un-empathetic, antisocial, cold and withdrawn, melancholy, difficulty breathing, heaviness in chest

When Excessive: poor boundaries, codependency, clingy, jealousy, narcissism, demanding

Physical Ailments When Blocked, Deficient, or Excessive: heart and lung issues, issues with arms, breasts, and thymus, shortness of breath, breathing issues, asthma, circulation issues

Throat Chakra

Name: *Vissudha* (purification)

Color: bright blue

Location In Body: throat, bronchial tubes, vocal cords, mouth, tongue, esophagus

Energy: speaking, communication

Element: ether

How It Influences Us: authenticity, truth, communication, self-expression, creativity

Physical Connections: throat area, bronchial tubes, vocal cords, lounge, mouth, esophagus

Qualities When Balanced: powerful, resonate and stable voice, good listener, effective communicator of thoughts and feelings, good timing and rhythm

When Blocked/Deficient: fear of speaking, soft and weak voice, shy, poor rhythm, inability to convey thoughts and feelings

When Excessive: too much talking, poor listener, gossipy, dominating, loud voice

Physical Ailments When Blocked, Deficient, or Excessive: sore throat, tight neck and shoulders, issues in the throat, ears, voice, and neck; jaw tension, toxicity

Third Eye or Brow Chakra

Name: *Ajna* (to perceive and command)

Color: purple/indigo

Location In Body: brow, forehead, between the eyes, the "third eye"

Energy: to see

Element: light

How It Influences Us: wisdom, imagination, intuition, vision

Physical Connections: eyes, brain, pituitary gland

Qualities When Balanced: intuitive, good memory, imaginative, perceptive, clear dreams and vision, clairvoyance

When Blocked/Deficient: headaches, issues with vision, poor memory, lack of imagination, nightmares, hallucinations

When Excessive: hallucinations, delusions, obsessions, nightmares

Physical Ailments When Blocked, Deficient, or Excessive: headaches, vision problems

Crown Chakra

Name: *Sahasrara* (thousandfold, thousand petals)

Color: violet

Location In Body: top of head

Energy: to know

Element: thought

How It Influences Us: connection, spiritual life, transcendence, divinity, vision

Physical Connections: spinal cord, cerebral cortex

Qualities When Balanced: enlightenment, intelligent, open-minded, wisdom, mastery, spiritually connected, ability to synthesize information

When Blocked/Deficient: learning difficulties, rigid belief systems, apathy

When Excessive: spiritually addicted, over-intellectualized

Physical Ailments When Blocked, Deficient, or Excessive: migraine headaches, brain tumors, amnesia

Body Armoring

"When the character pattern is predominately defensive in nature, we call it character armor, as it often thwarts the ability of the patient to become her best self, as well as compromises all aspects of life, including intimate relationships."
Patricia R. Frisch[20]

What is *body armoring*? The concept of body armoring is based on the fundamental research and methodologies of Wilhelm Reich, an eclectic and sometimes controversial Austrian doctor and psychoanalyst who lived in the first half of the twentieth century. Reich, a student and contemporary of Sigmund Freud, is considered one of the most radical and controversial figures in the field of psychiatry, pushing the bounds of acceptable thinking and acceptable practice. Reich is also credited with creating the field of bodywork[21], which has application to the field of coaching we are discussing in this book. It is his work in the body and, specifically, body armoring that we now will explore in our journey of coaching in, with, and through the body.

A foundational tenet in Reich's methodologies is that as human beings we have a life energy—or "orgone"—that flows through us as humans. If the energy flows unimpeded, Reich said, we as humans can fully experience life (much the same as the idea for chakras). For Reich, to be healthy meant that we could express ourselves both emotionally and sexually. As humans, though, we experience hardships and traumas as we grow from infancy into adulthood. As we experience hardships and trauma, our body develops armoring "bands" which impede life energy flowing through those areas of the body. The armoring can happen in the time of the event or the trauma and help us navigate the event. Or, if we are subject to the event or trauma for extended periods or events, our armoring can become set and part of our observer.

Another way to look at this: one can put on a helmet to deal with a specific event, but if the person continues to wear the helmet, it becomes part of their way of being. From a coaching perspective, we are interested in the armoring which has become part of the coachee's body, the armor that they wear full-time. This armoring numbs and protects us from feeling the intensity of strongly embodied emotions. In this book we will not go deep into the ins and outs of Reich's theories; rather, we simply want to set this as a foundation for the idea of armoring.

It is through different modalities—i.e., therapy or coaching, specifically somatic coaching in, with, or through the body—that individuals can release their armoring. As a result, this can allow the flow of energy or life energy, creating a more whole and healthier individual. Where there is armoring there will be muscles that have been contracted for extended periods of time. Because of this, sometimes the only way to deal with the armoring is through direct physical manipulation of the engaged muscle. We will explore this more in the section of this book dealing with how to coach in, with, and through the body armoring.

Reich believed that armoring in the body happens in seven main segments of the body. All of the sections are somewhat interrelated, and to release the armoring in one section may also require the releasing of the armoring in another section. As an additional note, the armoring can be more pronounced on one side or the other of the body in those sections. Let's go through the seven sections.

- **Eye/Ocular**: includes the top of the head, the forehead, the eyes, cheeks, and ears, to the base of the skull

- **Jaw and Mouth/Oral**: mouth and jaw

- **Throat and Neck/Cervical**: throat and neck

- **Thoracic**: shoulders, chest, upper back, arms, and hands; internally, it includes the heart

- **Waist/Diaphragmatic**: includes the diaphragm, and because of the diaphragm's effect on breathing, it includes the lungs

- **Belly/Abdominal**: stomach and other internal organs such as the liver, kidneys, and intestines

- **Pelvic (Including Legs)**: genitals and legs

We will explore each of these segments. As we do, we will also explore the following:

- Body parts and organs associated with each segment

- The biological processes which happen in that segment

- How the segment affects the flow of energy in the body

- How the segment manifests in the body

- Moods and emotions associated with the different segments

- How the armoring in each respective segment can affect individuals as they navigate the world

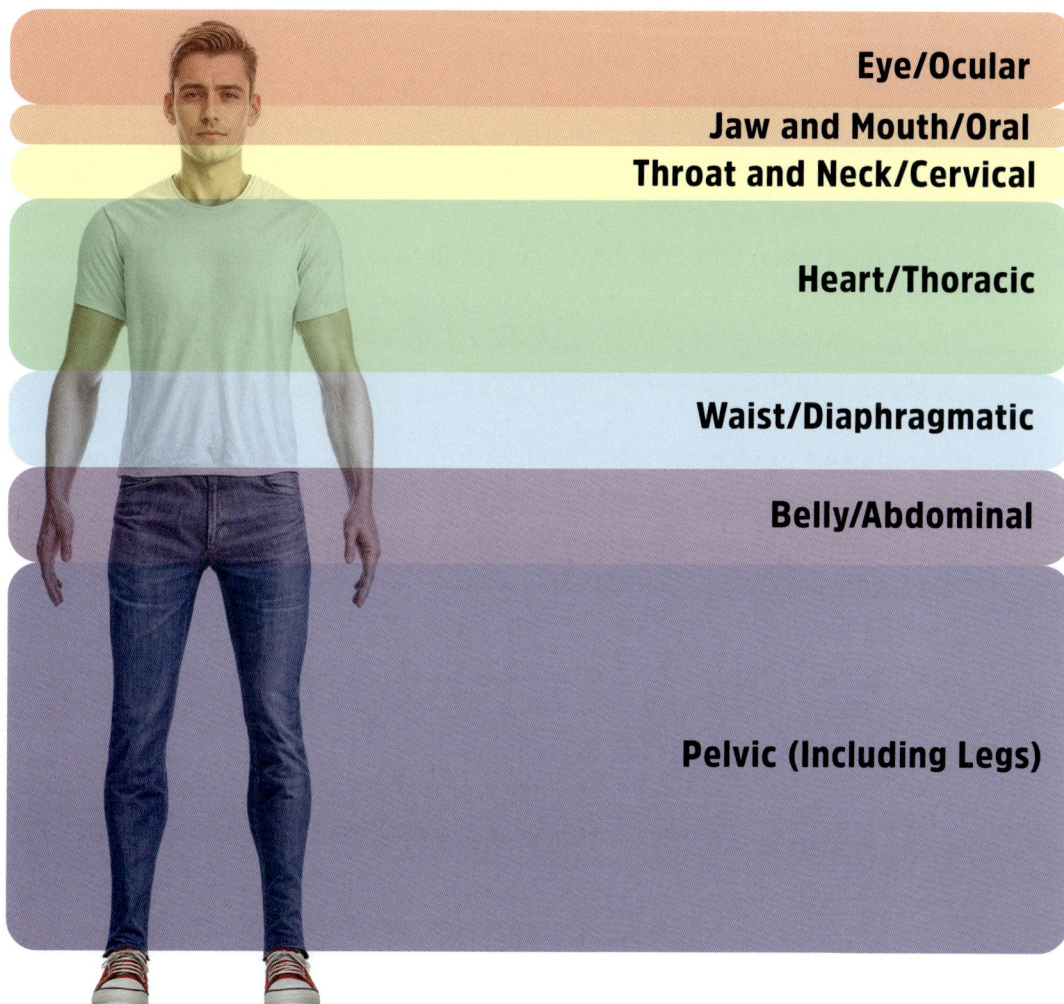

Eye/Ocular

Jaw and Mouth/Oral

Throat and Neck/Cervical

Heart/Thoracic

Waist/Diaphragmatic

Belly/Abdominal

Pelvic (Including Legs)

The Ocular Band / Eye

Eye/Ocular

- **Body Parts and Organs Associated with the Ocular Band**: includes the top of the head, the scalp, the forehead, and eyes, cheeks, ears, to the base of the skull

- **The Biological Processes That Occur in the Ocular Band**: sight, hearing, and smell

- **How the Armoring in the Ocular Band Affects the Flow of Energy in the Body**: Since this part of the body holds the brain, and in effect our thoughts, this is where we see the world from. For some it is the center of thinking, the place we operate from. The ocular band, in other words, is where "I" live. However, due to the armoring in this section of the body, a common breakdown is disconnection from other parts of the body. This is where people who "live in their heads" spend much of their body awareness, cut off from the rest of their bodies, many times especially from their "hearts."

- **How the Ocular Band Manifests in the Body**: The forehead is flat and not moving. The eyes are unable to open wide, and it appears as if they are squinting or focused. However, the armoring prevents really seeing with the eyes. The face seems more stoic and expressionless. A person with armoring in this area seems to be void of emotions.

- **Moods and Emotions Associated with the Ocular Band**: Due to the energy spent in thinking, there is limited emotion associated with the ocular band. Since there is armoring in the eyes, the ability to express emotions through the ocular band is very limited. The limitedness of the eye band means the body does not easily express emotions through crying, and those with ocular armoring do not regularly show sadness or laughter. However, there is the possibility of resentment, anger, worry, and indifference as emotional states.

- **How the Armoring in the Ocular Band Can Affect Individuals as They Navigate the World**: Eye issues such as short- or longsightedness can affect the ocular band. Headaches are also common ocular armoring due to the tension in the facial and eye muscles. Sinus and eye issues such as sinusitis and sties are common.

The Oral Band / Jaw and Mouth

- **Body Parts and Organs Associated with the Oral Band**: includes the mouth and jaw, the top of the throat and tonsils, the lips and teeth

Jaw and Mouth/Oral

- **The Biological Processes Which Occur in the Oral Band**: eating, swallowing, and the ability to produce sounds, whether speaking, yelling, laughing, or screaming. Along with sound is the ability to release emotions in the form of sound.

- **How the Armoring in the Oral Band Affects the Flow of Energy in the Body**: It is in the oral band that emotions are expressed sonically. The ability to fully express emotions is tied to the ability to fully allow them to leave the body as sound. The armoring of the jaw can limit the intensity and clarity of the emotions being expressed. Oral armoring causes emotions to be muted when expressed, and therefore limited. With this "gate" kept closed, it means one's energy is trapped in the body and not allowed to be expressed.

- **How the Oral Band Manifests in the Body**: The emotions expressed by individuals with oral armoring will be limited, and therefore the voice will be void or limited of vocal tone and expression. Facial expressions will be limited—a slight smile or expression—but overall, the jaw will be more tight and set. Because of the tight jaw there will be a restrained, more monotone voice.

- **Moods and Emotions Associated with the Oral Band**: Due to the "gatekeeping" of the jaw, moods and emotions will likely be limited. However, emotions that are likely to show up are anger and resentment. These emotions show up in a tense face that is focused, but the anger will show through.

- **How the Armoring in the Oral Band Can Affect Individuals as They Navigate the World**: A common medical malady associated with the jaw is migraine headaches. This armoring can also show up with tooth and gum issues related to the suppression of emotions.

The Cervical Band / Throat and Neck

- **Body Parts and Organs Associated With the Cervical Band**: includes the whole of the throat, including the tongue down

- **The Biological Processes Which Occur in the Cervical Band**: swallowing and the expression of emotions from the core of the body

- **How the Armoring in the Cervical Band Affects the Flow of Energy in the Body**: For the emotions and energy of the body to be able to express themselves though the mouth and jaw, they must first travel through the narrow throat and neck. Because of this, it is easy for emotions and energy to be bound up and trapped in the neck and throat.

Throat & Neck/Cervical

- **How the Cervical Band Manifests in the Body**: As the neck blocks energy and emotions, it becomes stiff as it stops both the emotions of the body escaping via the mouth and eyes and, at the same time, also stops a person from connecting with her or his body. This narrow passage then becomes a traffic jam in the body.

- **Moods and Emotions Associated with the Cervical Band**: In the throat anger can be "swallowed" and not allowed to escape. There is also the element of stubbornness around not showing emotion in the neck and throat.

- **How the Armoring in the Cervical Band Can Affect Individuals as They Navigate the World**: Coughing, frequent swallowing, the feeling of a lump, and even a frequency to touch or hide the throat when speaking in the throat area, are all common indicators of armoring in the throat.

The Thoracic Band / Heart

- **Body Parts and Organs Associated With the Thoracic Band**: The most prevalent organs associated with the thoracic band are the heart and lungs. Also associated with this band are the muscles of the chest and chest cage, shoulders, arms, hands, and upper back. Simply, it is the upper chest region of the body.

- **The Biological Processes Which Occur in the Thoracic Band**: Breathing, and the flow of blood in the body, are the main biological processes associated with the thoracic band.

Heart/Thoracic

- **How the Armoring in the Thoracic Band Affects the Flow of Energy in the Body**: Obviously, breathing and the flow of blood are two of the most fundamental biological processes for a human to be alive, and because of that, armoring in the thoracic band hinders and stops one from fully expressing themselves as humans. To breathe and feel in the heart are what it means to be alive, and if that is limited, the richness and intensity of life are diminished. It is in these areas that life should be fully expressed. To be in love, to experience deep sadness, to experience joy—all are in the thoracic band, and to unlock this band is the way to open the emotional well of being human. It is also in this area that to be blocked means to be kept from loving and contacting other human beings.

It is also through breathing in the thoracic band where aliveness comes. To breathe itself is one way; as humans we can open ourselves to others and feel. To be constricted in breathing means to be constricted in our ability to move and navigate the world around us. The athlete who takes deep and unrestricted breaths can elevate to heights never achieved. To be defeated is to be constricted in our abilities to breathe.

- **How the Thoracic Band Manifests in the Body**: Simply, the more the thoracic band is constricted, the more one's ability to feel different emotions and to experience the thrill and ups and downs of life are constricted. One can love so much that it hurts, and one can feel so unloved that it hurts. The armoring in this region allows the feelings to be numbed and limited. This can manifest in either self-control and restraint, or it can be shown in the numbness of not being able to experience strong moods and emotions.

- **Moods and Emotions Associated with the Thoracic Band**: All moods and emotions can be associated with the thoracic band. The key differentiator is not so much the mood or emotion but rather the intensity in which the mood or emotion is experienced and felt. When the thoracic band is unrestricted one can feel intense emotions ranging from rage, anger, and resentment to the other end of the spectrum: emotions such as love, joy, gratitude, and contentment. When thoracic armoring is limited, there will be movement in the band as one laughs, cries, and experiences intense emotions. Conversely, when there is armoring there will be limited emotions.

- **How the Armoring in the Thoracic Band Can Affect Individuals as They Navigate the World**: There can be diseases and ailments associated with the band such as chronic coughs, asthma, heart issues, and "a broken heart."

The Diaphragmatic Band / Waist

- **Body Parts and Organs Associated With the Diaphragmatic Band**: The actual diaphragm, a large muscle which separates the upper torso with the lungs and heart from the internal organs of the stomach, liver, pancreas, kidneys, and intestines, among others. The organs just below the diaphragm, the internal organs of the stomach, liver, pancreas, kidneys, and intestines, among others, are considered part of the diaphragmatic band.

Waist/Diaphragmatic

- **The Biological Processes Which Occur in the Diaphragmatic Band**: The diaphragm is the muscle, through how we breath, that expands and contracts to fill the lungs with oxygen and expel carbon dioxide on the other end of the contraction.

- **How the Armoring in the Diaphragmatic Band Affects the Flow of Energy in the Body**: Armoring in the diaphragmatic band causes the body to separate the belly and the lower half of the body from the upper chest and head of the body. Because of this, when there is armoring in the diaphragmatic band, there will be a separation between the energy of the lower bands and the abdominal/pelvic, which hinders the body's ability to tap those energies.

- **How the Diaphragmatic Band Manifests in the Body**: When the diaphragmatic band is constricted and armored, the ability to breath and experience the power of the upper chest is severely limited and, with it, the ability to experience or express those strong emotions.

- **Moods and Emotions Associated with the Diaphragmatic Band**: Armoring of the diaphragmatic band can cause one to freeze in their emotions and not be able to act in accordance with what they are experiencing. Also, intense rage is held in the diaphragmatic band.

- **How Armoring in the Diaphragmatic Band Can Affect Individuals as They Navigate the World:** Stomach issues such as nausea, gall bladder disease, upset stomach, liver conditions, and diabetes are associated with the diaphragmatic band.

The Abdominal Band / Belly

- **Body Parts and Organs Associated With the Abdominal Band**: Abdominal muscles, stomach, and lower back muscles are associated with the abdominal band.

- **The Biological Processes That Occur in the Abdominal Band**: digestion and waste elimination

- **How the Armoring in the Abdominal Band Affects the Flow of Energy in the Body**: The abdominal band is the location of the "gut"—and therefore intuition and unexpressed feelings.

Belly/Abdominal

- **How the Abdominal Band Manifests in the Body**: When the abdominal band is armored up, there is a restriction of unexpressed feelings, desires, and emotions. When the band is released and flowing, there is the ability to release and eliminate repressed feelings.

- **Moods and Emotions Associated with the Abdominal Band**: tiredness and the repression of moods such as anger, grief, and fear

- **How Armoring in the Abdominal Band Can Affect Individuals as They Navigate the World**: stomach and intestinal issues

The Pelvic Band / Pelvis and Legs

- **Body Parts and Organs Associated With the Pelvic Band:** Our sexuality is in the pelvic band, as this is the location of our genitals. Our legs and feet are also in this band.

- **The Biological Processes Which Occur in the Pelvic Band:** procreating, along with walking and standing

- **How the Armoring in the Pelvic Band Affects the Flow of Energy in the Body:** Since the pelvis is the location of the legs, how we walk and navigate the world lives in this band. This is also where we relate to the ground and our sense of groundedness. When our legs are strong and flexible, we can nimbly move through the world. When they are tense and rigid, we methodically plod through the world. When the pelvic band is freed, we are more free, sexually, to experiment, allowing for enjoyment and pleasure.

Pelvic (Including Legs)

- **How the Pelvic Band Manifests in the Body**: When there is rigidity and armoring in the pelvic band, individuals are more uptight and disconnected from the ground. A lack of armoring in this band allows for a more vibrant self in both the domain of sexuality and connectedness to the ground.

- **Moods and Emotions Associated with the Pelvic Band**: Fear and rage are held in the pelvic band.

- **How Armoring in the Pelvic Band Can Affect Individuals As They Navigate the World:** sexual issues, and issues in the legs

Body Armoring: Final Thought for Now

Allow me a last thought, as we end this chapter, on body armoring. Many times one's body armor can be extremely powerful and so embodied that the armor will do what it is designed to do and deflect attempts to lessen it. Therefore, many times it takes specific modalities to deal with issues. Those modalities can range into the therapeutic realm and may no longer reside in the domain of coaching, but instead come through therapy. However, there are practices like somatic body work which function along with the armoring that remain in the domain of coaching. We will return to somatic body work later in this book.

A *Liquid Accordion* in Action

The Body in Language Continues

More of the body in language and figures of speech. When we talk . . .

• we can bite our tongue

• we can speak tongue-in-cheek

• we can speak at the top of our lungs

Back to the body as a whole. In our everyday speech, we can get (or be):

• in shape

• on someone's nerves

• our ass in gear

• an earful

• something off our chest

• in over our head

• a frog in our throat

• our hands tied

ELEVEN

Archetypes and Bodies

"The soul is the same in all living creatures, although the body of each is different."
Hippocrates

Chances are that as someone who might be interested in the topic of coaching in, with, and through the body, you have at some point come across one or more theories or assessments that investigate different archetypes of people. In addition, chances are the assessment has a root in one of four different types for that assessment.

Some of the many examples of four styles:

- **The Four Temperaments**: Greek physicians Hippocrates (460–370 BC) and, later, Galen (129–216 AD) developed and explored the concept of the four temperaments. This psychological theory explored the idea that there are four fundamental human personality types. The four types, they said, are affected by four body fluids, and these fluids affect one's personality and behaviors. The four temperaments are *phlegmatic, melancholic, choleric,* and *sanguine.*

- **Four Archetypes**: Swiss psychologist Carl Jung (1875-1961) developed, among other theories, the idea of the four archetypes of human behavior. The four archetypes are *mother, rebirth, spirit,* and *trickster.* This has led to many evolutions of his theories, including:

- **The Archetypes of the Mature Masculine**: the king, the warrior, the magician, and the lover

- **In the Indigenous People of North America are the Traditions of Four Ways of Being**: the warrior, the teacher, the healer, and the visionary

- In the 1950s through 1970s Roger Reid and David Merrill developed the behavioral-based Social Styles™, which investigated four basic behavioral styles in human interactions. This program, based on research from the Department of the U.S. Navy and Ohio State University, explored how individuals have basic patterns of behaviors and interpersonal behaviors which can be identified and agreed upon. Inherent in each of the styles is a body shape that aligns with other methodologies. These four styles are:
    - Driving
    - Expressive
    - Analytical
    - Amiable

- Multiple others, all with some variation of four, include:
    - 4 directions: north, east, west, and south
    - 4 elements: water, fire, air, and earth
    - 4 seasons: fall, winter, spring, and summer
    - 4 animals: lions, beavers, otters, and golden retrievers
    - 4 colors: green, blue, yellow, orange
    - DiSC(r): (D)ominance, (i)nfluence, (S)teadiness, and (C)onscientiousness

- In a white paper produced by The Newfield Network and Mauricio Gonzalez, the authors proposed that there are four basic body dispositions that show up in humans as we navigate the world. These four dispositions are determination, openness, flexibility, and stability. The paper provides an overview of the body dispositions and how they manifest in the body and emotions.

Some of these theories are more personality based, while some are behavior based. Most, if not all, of the various assessments/theories of the body are minimized or nonexistent. If they are referenced, it is more as an afterthought than a way of observing others. ***Missing in most is the foundational idea that it is the body shape itself that is the foundation for how one observes the world: change the body, change how we see the world.*** Our aim is to integrate and combine many of the "four types" into a visual and understandable typology as a place to start to observe to better coach in, with, and through the body.

For now, let's just explore the four basic body shapes.

The Four Basic Body Shapes

"The body you have is the body you live."
Graf Durckheim[22]

A Brief Introduction to the Four Basic Body Shapes

I have attempted to integrate/consolidate the themes and somatic applicabilities of many of the different assessments into what we define as the four basic body shapes. These shapes are a basic way that individuals approach and navigate the world and are a place to explore for understanding. It is possible that you have knowledge or awareness of some of the different assessments, and some of what is shared here might not fit exactly to how you understand your particular assessment. My request is to explore these with openness and curiosity, and as you start coaching in, with, and through the body, try them on for size.

A Few Key Points About the Four Basic Body Shapes

There Is No Right or Wrong Shape. All the shapes influence how we see the world, and whatever shape we are in the moment determines what we see as possibilities in the world. *Although there is no right or wrong shape, there can be effective and ineffective* *behaviors associated with each of the shapes.* The shape of a person in the moment can lead to better—or at least not as good—outcomes. The applicability of this to coaching is that we as humans have shapes that both support and limit our potential results. It goes back to the idea of the Observer-Action-Results (OAR) model. This shows itself in our Shape (Observer)-Actions-Results.

Although We Show Four Basic Shapes, We Are Never Wholly One Shape at a Time, Nor Does the Shape We Are in Stay Static and Fixed. Rather we are, as the title of this book suggests, a liquid accordion, ever changing, expanding and contracting. However, the idea we put forth is that over time we start to spend more and more of our time shaped in a particular way. This becomes our shape over time, and whatever shape we are in in the moment is the shape we are bringing to the conversation we are in.

As we explore each shape, we will follow a similar outline for each, and that will include the following: overview of the basic body shape, a few overall paragraphs describing that style/shape, and how it shows up in the world. Paragraphs will include:

- Overview

- Overall somatic shape

- Behaviors/descriptors of this shape

- How this shape serves the observer

- Shadow/downsides of this shape

- Other descriptors/names used by various assessments associated with this basic body style

Actual Body: Slides/images are included. We'll show visual representations of each of the four basic body shapes. They include:

1) Overall body shape/range of motion/energy. This image will give the broad overview of what to expect with this basic body shape.

2) Facial expressions: common facial expressions of this basic body shape

3) Hand usage: what hand gestures/usages are associated with this basic body shape

4) Eye contact: how the eyes are used by this basic body shape

5) Behaviors: common behaviors seen and associated with the basic body shape. These include:
   - Relation to time
   - Problem-solving
   - What happens when this basic body shape comes under pressure

- How this basic body shape uses humor

- How this basic body shape may dress

- Moods/emotions expressed by this basic body shape

6) Speaking: what you might hear when interacting with this basic body shape. These include:

- Word choice/usage: actual words you will likely hear when this basic body shape is in a conversation

- Voice: what you will notice in this shape's voice—things such as volume, tone, pace of speech, inflection, quantity of speech

The four basic body shapes, then, in no particular order, are:

1) The Results Shape

2) The Spontaneous Shape

3) The Amiable Shape

4) The Methodical Shape

The *Liquid Accordion* in Action « « « « « « « «

The human body has more than six hundred different identified muscles! Whether talking, typing an email, or throwing a ball, there are countless combinations of the expansion and contraction of the liquid accordion that allow us as humans to navigate our world.

The Results Body Shape

"Our life always expresses the result of our dominant thoughts."
Soren Kierkegaard

As the name implies, the *results body shape* is a body that is shaped toward producing results. Whether it be the completion of a task, the winning of an argument, the desire to get from point A to point B, or the literal winning of a battle, this shape allows the individual to focus his or her energy and being on getting things done—now. To facilitate results, this body is designed for action and is focused on the point at hand. The eyes focus on what is present to get to the end. The muscles of a results body are tensed and armored so that, as the body moves forward, obstacles and challenges can be either brushed out of the way, quickly bypassed, or possibly even rolled over with sheer force.

The energy is forward and ratcheted up to the needed level to achieve success. The results body is the body of a warrior, of an athlete driving to the goal line or finish line, of a parent defending his or her child. All the energy is for one outcome, one set of results, for success. This success, which can be hard-fought, does not come for free, though. In its path are the casualties of the desire to win, a fallen opponent, a damaged relationship, bruised friendships. This shape allows for victory and, in the end, many times, bridges are burned that cannot be repaired.

» » » » » » »
The *Liquid Accordion* in Action

Still More of The Body in Language

The body is frequently being used in language—and as a sort of language unto itself.

We can:
- pick someone's brain
- be a bundle of nerves
- bend over backwards
- breathe easier
- eat, sleep, and breathe something
- go behind someone's back
- jump down someone's throat
- lose our nerve
- rub elbows with others
- smell blood in the water
- toe the line
- work our butt off
- carry the team on our shoulders
- face reality
- not face reality
- mend our broken heart
- carry the load
- shoulder a burden
- lose face
- think off the top of our head
- see face to face
- let our hair down
- tear our hair out
- split hairs
- play it by ear
- take it on the chin
- learn something by heart
- sing our heart out
- stick our neck out
- stand shoulder to shoulder
- cover our ass
- be at someone's throat
- raise eyebrows
- hold our breath

The actual somatic shape of the results body shape is a body full of muscular tension. Starting with the head, we see a face that comes across with a scowl, a look of anger and frustration. The forehead is tensed, the jaw steeled, the eyes focused. The core of the body has tension as if the wearer has a plate of chest and body armor, which keeps feelings and obstacles at bay. The body leans forward, causing the muscles in the body to work overtime to battle, fighting gravity wanting to pull it over. The arms and legs are moving, but not in an inefficient manner. Rather, they are utilized to get results: a quick email dashed off, a direct point made with the hands moving, or a brisk walk down the hall to the next meeting. The body can be described as hard, intense, action-oriented, and focused.

Behaviors associated with the results body shape are action-oriented and moving toward the objective. This can range from intense focus on a data spreadsheet—hands quickly typing to create an outcome—to full movement toward an objective, all parts of the body in harmony to the result. While in a results body shape, a person can be oblivious to what they deem irrelevant data. Another person's smile, conversations, and actions can be missed as the body does not see these things as leading to success.

This shape serves the observer as it allows for success and the completion of tasks from the task list (whether that list is written or not). People who navigate life in a results body shape tend to get many things done. They have order in their world, and this is the result of them taking action and not idling away their time.

The downside, or shadow side, of the results body shape is the damage done due to the lack of awareness of others' needs or feelings. Taking massive action can be great for one's own needs, but many times the needs of others get neglected or run over. Hurt feelings in others, damaged relationships, and a callousness to the effects of taking action are all shadow sides of this body shape. Also, another challenge to someone who lives in the results body shape is that there may not be time in all of the taking of action to take care of one's own self and vulnerabilities.

When we can't access the results body shape we cannot effectively navigate toward results, and our body is too affected by the challenges and struggles to move forward. We give up easily and are more concerned with harmony with others than the results needed.

Some of the descriptors used regarding the results body shape:

Positive Descriptors

- Leader

- Proactive

- Results-driven

- Producer

- Go-Getter

Negative Descriptors

- "Jerk"

- Uncaring

- Callous

- Mean

- Arrogant

- Self-serving

- "A$$ hole"

Other Assessment Names

- Resolute

- Warrior

- Driver

- Driving

- Type A

Overall Body Shape/Range of Motion/Energy/Locations of Tension

The Results Body Shape

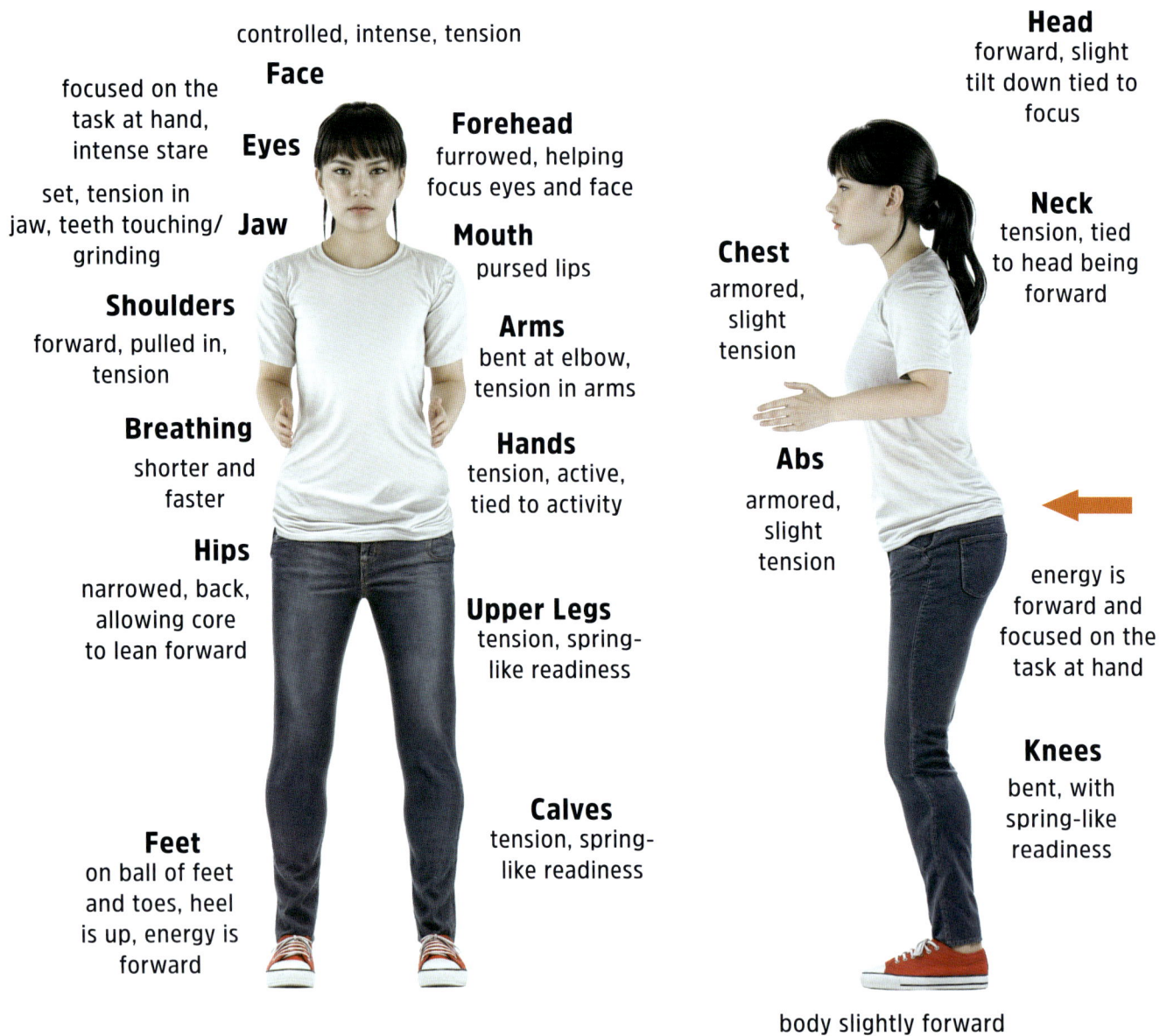

controlled, intense, tension

Face

focused on the task at hand, intense stare

Eyes

set, tension in jaw, teeth touching/ grinding

Jaw

Shoulders

forward, pulled in, tension

Breathing

shorter and faster

Hips

narrowed, back, allowing core to lean forward

Feet

on ball of feet and toes, heel is up, energy is forward

Forehead

furrowed, helping focus eyes and face

Mouth

pursed lips

Arms

bent at elbow, tension in arms

Hands

tension, active, tied to activity

Upper Legs

tension, spring-like readiness

Calves

tension, spring-like readiness

Head

forward, slight tilt down tied to focus

Neck

tension, tied to head being forward

Chest

armored, slight tension

Abs

armored, slight tension

energy is forward and focused on the task at hand

Knees

bent, with spring-like readiness

body slightly forward

Additional Behaviors/Markers of the Results Body Shape

Facial Expression: Shows up as an angry, focused face. Visible tension in the jaw, eyes, and forehead. Furled forehead, focused eyes, clenched jaw.

Body Posture/Energy: The body is leaning forward, both standing and sitting. Eyes, head, and hands are focused on the action at hand. Energy is *forward*.

Range/Speed of Motion/Walking: Body movement is forward and on the faster side of pace. Walking is brisk and "going somewhere." Movements are geared toward actions and are efficient. There are few to very little unneeded movements.

Hands: Very crisp, and forceful movements. You see the ends of the hands, the back of the hands, fingers pointing. The person remains in the core of the body; often, double hand movement in tandem.

Eyes: focused on the task at hand, intense stare; moves when/where the focus moves

Voice: firm and resolute voice, more monotone, but with a tone of intensity and possible anger

Speaking pace: faster
Volume: even volume, more on the loud side, adjusting to conviction of point
Firmness: quite firm

Speaking: Direct, to the point, efficient speaking. May dominate conversation, and when speaking words are short and to the point. Relevant task, facts, and data.

Word Use: more "black and white" words: "yes/no," "always/never," "right/wrong"

Speech—Subjects, Inflections, Descriptives:

Subject of speech: tasks
Inflection: slight
Descriptives: facts/data

Time, Problem-solve, 5W+H:

Relation to time: present, very time-sensitive/driven, time is money
Problem-solve: linear, key decision points, success is the focus
5 W+H: what, when, where

Humor, Clothing:

Humor: biting, cynical
Clothing: one notch above the norm; more formal, power colors (red, black, gray, silver)

The Results Body Shape: Famous People and Characters

Famous people and characters with the results body shape can be identified by their very direct comments and no-nonsense way of being. They sometimes make controversial statements, but, at the same time, do not seem to fret about what other people think.

Many of the famous people you will instantly know, but perhaps you have not read or studied a great deal about them. Even a small bit of research will show you why they are chosen for this list. For the characters list of my examples of these different body shapes. I have chosen four iconic TV or movie series, from the more recent (*Yellowstone*) to the silly (though wildly popular, *The Simpsons.)* Notice, with *Seinfeld*, how each of the four main characters embody one of the types. The last one I chose is a TV and movie series that has endured for six decades: *Star Trek*. The characters from each illustrate the point.

Famous people

Hillary Clinton	Kim Kardashian
Donald Rumsfeld	Richard Nixon
Megan Markle	Michael Jordan
Dick Cheney	Tiger Woods
Malcolm X	
Candace Owens	
Saddam Hussein	

Characters

Elaine (*Seinfeld*)	Rip Wheeler (*Yellowstone*)
Mr. Burns (*The Simpsons*)	Captain Kirk (*Star Trek*)
John Dutton (*Yellowstone*)	

The Spontaneous Body Shape

"Dancing: the highest intelligence in the freest body."
Isadora Duncan[23]

The *spontaneous body shape* allows one to go wherever the situation calls. It allows for laughter, a change in direction, swift action, spontaneity. This body shape allows one to do whatever the owner deems necessary in the moment. This change in direction can influence others and bring the user to the center of attention. This body shape, though, can also create challenges. When this body is up, it can be *way* up and brings things alive; and when it is down, it can be *way* down and brings others with it. The challenge for the spontaneous body shape is the happy medium: finding the ability to not be the center of attention, to not be the one talking, to not be the one laughing, to not be moving—these realities can be a challenge for this body shape. It is the body of a joker, of the comedian or actor bringing the audience along for the emotional ride. Sometimes this body shape serves to have the right thing to say, the right emotion to balance out a room. By contrast, though, sometimes this body shape impulsively says the wrong thing, is overly dramatic, is too spontaneous for the situation.

The actual somatic shape of the spontaneous body shape is ever changing and almost always in motion. Even when it is not in motion, the shape has an effect on others, as if they are on a roller coaster and the coaster has suddenly stopped—that is, until it quickly moves again. The face of the spontaneous body shape is varied and animated. The term "poker face" does not apply to this face, as the face shifts from emotions as varied as happiness and anger to frustration. This face does not stay still, either. Another clue in this body shape is the hands are almost always in motion. The more the passion around a subject, the more the hands and related areas are moving to tell the size of the story, or to emphasize the main points. The body itself can be very flexible, and this shows up in a walk that is all over the place, rarely in a straight line. The body can be described as fluid, flexible, dramatic, and in action.

Behaviors associated with the spontaneous body shape are movement-focused and seemingly without a rhythm or a sustained, unified direction. This can range from telling an animated story to others to seemingly being bored moments later while listening to the other person talking. While this body can add energy to a conversation, its shadow side can seem self-centered and suck the energy out of a conversation. A theme in the behavior of this shape is movement—but not sustained movement. Instead, movement that is variable, hard to follow.

This shape serves the observer as it allows for the ability to use powerful emotions to bring full energy to a task or relationship. When this shape is prevalent the utilizer is moving toward an objective with passion and energy.

The downside, or shadow side, of the spontaneous body shape is the drain on the emotional energy of others. The roller coaster of emotions and body movement—perhaps useful and amusing at first—can be, after a time, draining and tiring to others. Many times this shape struggles with the down-the-middle emotions and not being the center of attention or not being the person talking. Others can quickly tire of these "antics" or "all the drama." Here is a way this shape can be perceived by others: as too much of a good thing.

The *Liquid Accordion* in Action

The Brain, Part 1

It is estimated that the average human brain contains more than 86 billion—that's billion, with b—nerve cells, and these are connected by more than 100 billion connections. Add them up and the number is greater than the total number of stars in the Milky Way galaxy.

The Brain, Part 2

Size doesn't matter. The average brain weighs about 3 pounds. Men's brains tend to be larger than women's. Before you get too big-headed, though, men, there is no correlation between brain size and intelligence.

When We Can't Access Spontaneous Body Shape

When we can't access the spontaneous body shape, we are limited in the ability to access emotions. This means we may not be able to get "fired up" for something, or may be unable to bring a different speed to a situation. This can mean that we are going too fast or too slow, and not able to shift to the moment.

Some of the descriptors surrounding the spontaneous body shape:

Positive Descriptors

- Energetic
- Creative
- Cheerleader
- Motivator
- Visionary
- Vibrant
- Charismatic

Negative Descriptors

- Obnoxious
- Loud
- Self-serving
- "Too . . ." . . . too energetic, too creative, too vibrant, etc.
- Annoying
- Drama Queen/King
- Loose Cannon
- Maverick

Other Assessment Names

- Expressive
- Flexible
- Otter
- Joker

The *Liquid Accordion* in Action « « « « « « «

The Spontaneous Body Shape: Famous People and Characters

Famous people and characters with the spontaneous body shape are likely the easiest to identify because they make themselves known. They come across, at times, as opinionated and controversial. Social media is full of these types, people seeking to be seen.

Famous people

Kanye West	Lady Gaga	Ronald Reagan
Oprah Winfrey	Rush Limbaugh	Prince Harry
Robin Williams	Kathy Griffin	Donald Trump
Rosie O'Donnell	Bill Clinton	

Characters

Kramer (*Seinfeld*)	Beth Dutton (*Yellowstone*)
Homer Simpson (*The Simpsons*)	Dr. McCoy (*Star Trek*)
Bart Simpson (*The Simpsons*)	

Overall Body Shape/Range of Motion/Energy/Locations of Tension

The Spontaneous Body Shape

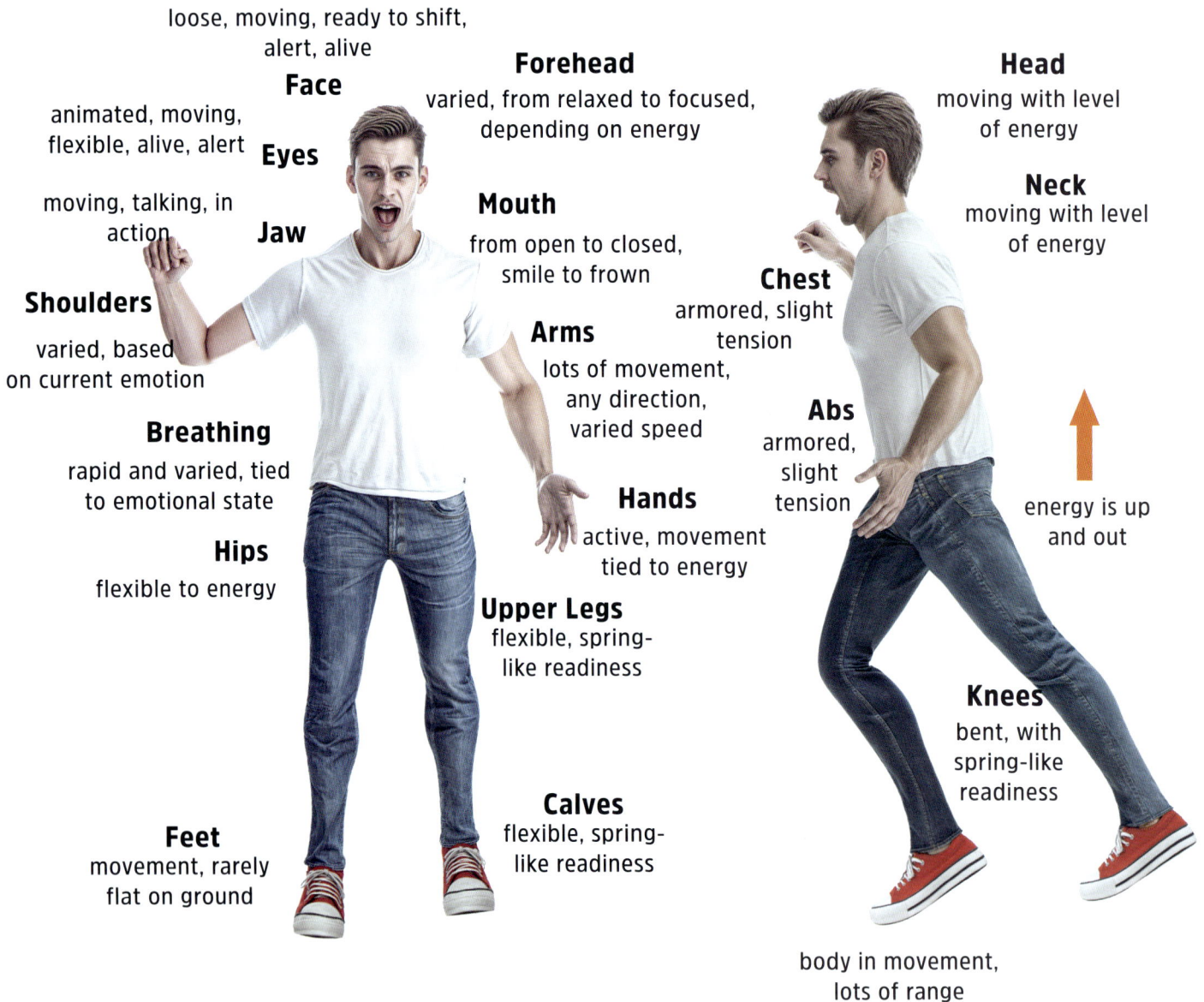

loose, moving, ready to shift, alert, alive

Face

animated, moving, flexible, alive, alert

Eyes

moving, talking, in action

Jaw

Shoulders

varied, based on current emotion

Breathing

rapid and varied, tied to emotional state

Hips

flexible to energy

Feet

movement, rarely flat on ground

Forehead

varied, from relaxed to focused, depending on energy

Mouth

from open to closed, smile to frown

Arms

lots of movement, any direction, varied speed

Hands

active, movement tied to energy

Upper Legs

flexible, spring-like readiness

Calves

flexible, spring-like readiness

Head

moving with level of energy

Neck

moving with level of energy

Chest

armored, slight tension

Abs

armored, slight tension

energy is up and out

Knees

bent, with spring-like readiness

body in movement, lots of range

Additional Behaviors/Markers of the Spontaneous Body Shape

Facial Expression: Animated face, which is tied to the emotional roller coaster that the person is on. If the person is sad, the face shows it; if they are happy, the face shows it, and so on.

Body Posture/Energy: The body is in motion, and so it can be up, down, in any direction. This body shape rides its emotions so the energy can run the whole spectrum. Energy is "up and out."

Range/Speed of Motion/Walking: Body movement is in action and forward, or side-to-side, wherever the energy takes the person. Walk is tied to the emotional state, from brisk and going somewhere to slow and melancholy. Movements are geared toward emotions and the story at play, and these movements can be very inefficient at times. Movement is most always present.

Hands: Of all the body shapes, this is the one most likely to use the hands—from small to big gestures, depending on the story and emotions involved. The person in this body shape uses hands to connect and give high-fives, hugs, fist bumps—all of these are very common.

Eyes: Focused, alert, and scanning for emotional data to determine where to take the conversation. The eyes tend to focus on where the emotional connection is.

Voice: Varied and animated. It is used as a tool to bring others along for the story.
Pace of voice: varied pace, but more on the faster side, especially when this shape is in action or in the midst of a story
Volume: louder, and a more varied volume of voice
Firmness: more on the firm side, but this can vary based on the story

Speaking: Opinionated and colorful speaking. May dominate conversations, and when speaking this person personalizes the story and puts themselves in the center of the story.

Word Use: more "black and white" words and more colorful words: "yes/no," "always/never," "right/wrong," "exhausted," "the best/the worst," "amazing," "phenomenal," and many more

Speech: Subjects, Inflections, Descriptives:
Subject of speech: people, personalization
Inflection: lots of inflection
Descriptives: opinions and stories

Time, Problem-solve, 5W+H:

Relation to time: future-oriented, very time sensitive if activity is not aligned with needs

Problem-solve: very much of a big-picture focus, then lots of action, but easily distracted or attracted to the next shiny thing

5 W+H: who

Humor, Clothing:

Humor: The most likely of the body shapes to use humor in all forms, including possibly inappropriate humor. The most likely to be laughing.

Clothing: Anything is possible. Clothing is tied to the story that this shape wants to live in. Most likely to push the boundaries of appropriateness of dress. Often dresses for effect.

FIFTEEN

The Amiable Body Shape

*"The most amiable people are those who least
wound the self-love of others."*
Jean de la Bruyere[24]

The *amiable body shape* is about open connection with other human beings. To be this person, the amiable body is open and accepting of those around him/her and willing to be vulnerable in interactions with others. This body shape is conducive to a smile, a nod of approval, and love for others. This is the body that cares about the needs of others over its own. This body serves one to be in intimate and emotional conversations and in the sharing of feelings and connectivity. Because this body is open and vulnerable, it leaves its owner susceptible to being hurt and disappointed from feelings not reciprocated, or from the emotional daggers of others. This body becomes a martyr and does not easily take a stand; rather, it suffers so that others do not. It is the body of the lover, the caregiver, the nurturer. This is a body which can be light on the touch and not overly intrusive to others. This body serves to help one be a great team player, a cheerleader, and a humble and willing servant to others.

The overall somatic shape of this body is one that is soft and inviting. The face of the amiable body shape is warm with a hint of a smile or other emotions to convey the necessary feelings in the moment. The eyes are soft and will connect with others who are also open and vulnerable, but will immediately turn away at the hint of anger or other perceived dangerous emotions. The arms of this body are open and the palms of the hands revealed to show no hidden agendas or threats. There are not overly fast movements—this is a desire to not have the body stand out—but rather there are slower, more methodical movements putting others at ease. A clue to this body is that it is likely to blend into the surroundings, with the only clue being a slight smile to put others at ease. This body can be described as warm, open, soft, loving, and huggable.

Behaviors associated with the amiable body style include playful and warm conversations, a smile to welcome others, and a pleasant hello to brighten the days of others. This body style will find itself in conversations which are safe and pleasant, and will likely desire to miss, or skip, conversations which might be considered offensive or critical of others. A theme in this shape is the desire for all to get along and work together. This body shape has the desire for harmony.

»»»»»»»» The *Liquid Accordion* in Action

Bad News, Good News

When it comes to the liquid accordion in action, there is both bad news and good news. Let's handle the bad news first: every three to four *seconds*, more than 50,000 cells die in our body. The good news: every three to four seconds, they are replaced.

This shape serves the observer as it allows him or her to take care of all others and provides a place of not only emotional safety and support, but also a place for others to see and be their best selves. The amiable body shape *serves others first*. Because of this, a great need for this shape is the need for trust. With trust in others, much can be done, but without trust there is the avoidance of the difficult things to be said.

This shape does have its shadow side, and that is the need for harmony and community, which many times leads to the inability to have difficult conversations or make difficult decisions.

When we can't access the amiable body shape, we miss out on the ability to love and be vulnerable. It is in the amiable shape that we welcome others into our world and love them with wholeness.

Let's look at some of the descriptors used to portray the amiable body shape.

Positive Descriptors

- Caring
- Loving
- Team player
- Cheerleader
- Supportive
- Open
- Pliable
- Warm

Negative Descriptors

- Too soft
- Touchy-feely
- Emotionally heavy
- Too nice

Other Assessment Names

- Amiable
- Open
- Lover
- Golden Retriever

Overall Body Shape/Range of Motion/Energy/Locations of Tension

The Amiable Body Shape

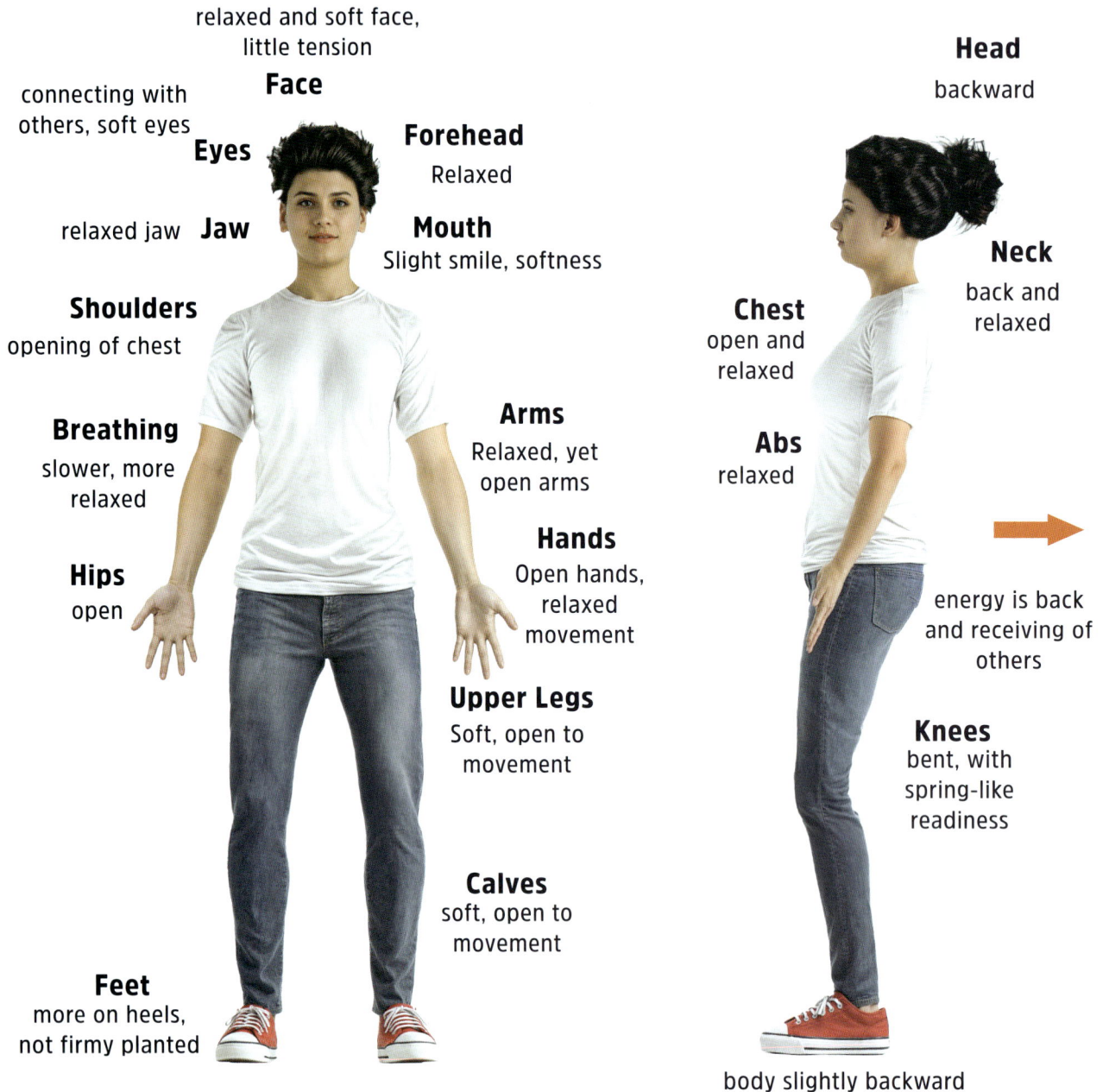

relaxed and soft face,
little tension
Face

connecting with
others, soft eyes
Eyes

Forehead
Relaxed

relaxed jaw **Jaw**

Mouth
Slight smile, softness

Shoulders
opening of chest

Breathing
slower, more
relaxed

Arms
Relaxed, yet
open arms

Hands
Open hands,
relaxed
movement

Hips
open

Upper Legs
Soft, open to
movement

Calves
soft, open to
movement

Feet
more on heels,
not firmy planted

Head
backward

Neck
back and
relaxed

Chest
open and
relaxed

Abs
relaxed

energy is back
and receiving of
others

Knees
bent, with
spring-like
readiness

body slightly backward

Additional Behaviors/Markers of the Amiable Body Shape

Facial Expression: A soft, inviting face which disarms others. Slight smile and a warmness and caring from the eyes. Can turn away from the slightest hint of tension with others.

Body Posture/Energy: The body is "back" and "open." The energy is about receiving others and being a safe place; it often provides a warm hug for others. This person is open to connectivity and intimacy.

Range/Speed of Motion/Walking: The body movement is about receiving and being open and vulnerable. Speed is on the slower side and not in bold, but relaxed, movements.

Hands: Most likely to see the palms of the hands as an open palm, showing no threats and conveying no vulnerability. This is the most likely of all the shapes to physically touch another in a way to connect.

Eyes: Relaxed and open to connecting; however, if another person's eyes show tension or perceived danger, then he or she is likely to turn the eyes away from the tension.

Voice: Soft and a slight inflection. Used as a tool to alert others that this shape is safe and caring.

> Pace of voice: slower, slight inflection
> Volume: on the quieter side; unlikely to use volume to make a point
> Firmness: more on the soft side, but can vary slightly based on the story

Speaking: Not opinionated when speaking with others unless there is trust to create. This body type does not seek to dominate conversations, but rather seeks to put others in the spotlight and keep conversation safe and flowing.

Word Use: more "gray" and pleasant words: "hello," "please," "if possible," "thank you," "that is so nice"

Speech: Subjects, Inflections, Descriptives:
> Subject of speech: people, personalization
> Inflection: subtle but present inflection
> Descriptives: opinions and stories

Time, Problem-Solve, 5W+H:
> Relation to time: present-oriented, very aware of how they affect the time of others
> Problem-solve: aware of how problem-solving will affect others and what the consequences of the actions will be
> 5 W+H: why

Humor, clothing:

Humor: safe humor; puns, silly, self-deprecating humor

Clothing: Very safe, comfortable; will be well within the boundaries of what is acceptable in their community. Likely, pastels and earth tones. Will wear uniform to fit in with, and show, connectivity. Will never wear potentially offensive clothing.

» » » » » » **The *Liquid Accordion* in Action**

The Amiable Body Shape: Famous People and Characters

Famous people with the amiable body shape are not likely to be front and center; rather, they have a reputation of being extremely nice, even caring, of others. This person comes across as someone who would treat his or her fans with respect and take time for them.

Famous people

Dolly Parton	Bob Newhart
Garth Brooks	Paula Abdul
Betty White	

Characters

George Costanza (*Seinfeld*)	Marge Simpson (*The Simpsons*)
Ned Flanders (*The Simpsons*)	Mr. Scott ("Scotty") (*Star Trek*)

SIXTEEN

The Methodical Body Shape

"The body is the outermost layer of the mind."
David Mitchell[25]

The *methodical body shape* is about stability and methodically approaching the world from a predictable perspective. Those with this body shape strive to create a known and safe world. This is a body shape which is not into relationships for deep interpersonal connection but rather for the ability to access the other person for information or as part of a process. This body shape is conducive to a formal relationship with others. This is the body that cares about an organized world, a world with a place for everything and in which change is minimized. This body shape serves to analyze data and create processes to maintain an orderly world. Because this body is so stable, it does not do well with change and struggles to be flexible and adaptable. When there is conflict, this body shape deals with the tension by avoiding it. This person is good at being "the ostrich with its head in the sand," looking and walking the other way when conflict arises. It is the body of the king or queen, methodically keeping all well in the kingdom by maintaining the status quo. This is the body that keeps things stable and safe.

The somatic shape of this body is, overall, one that is stiff and unmoving. The body is a vessel for travel and action. The face of the methodical body shape is unemotional and can come across as stoic or cold. The eyes are focused on the task at hand but not intense. The arms of this body shape are down at the side or in action with the task at hand, but there is very little unnecessary movement. It goes along at a slower, more methodical pace. A clue to this body is that it is likely to blend into the surroundings, only standing out through its lack of movement or its visual showing of emotions. This body can be described as formal, rigid, and inflexible.

Behaviors associated with the methodical body style include those movements aligned with the task at hand. If the person is working at the computer, that is all the movement one will likely see. This body shape will be in conversations which are formal and, at times, a bit uncomfortable for others. A theme in this shape is *efficiency in taking action.* The desire to be correct lives in this body.

This shape serves the observer as it allows the person to methodically navigate the world around them. Because of this, this observer is likely not to be in small talk or drama and stories, but rather in task and process. This shape allows for a world that is organized and formal, one that is free from the ups and downs of the emotions of others. With the ability to be methodical, we gain learning from repetition.

The shadow side of the methodical body shape is the lack of flexibility to adapt quickly to situations. The need for tried and true, proven methodologies leaves its owner adrift if the situation is rapidly changing or in flux. This shape struggles with the unknown and the emotions of others.

Here are some of the descriptors used to explain the methodical body shape.

Positive Descriptors

- Methodical
- Predictable
- Stable
- Task-focused
- Detailed-oriented
- Problem-solver

Negative Descriptors

- Stoic
- Stiff
- Formal
- Uncaring
- Cold
- Mechanical
- Boring
- Not personable

Other Assessment Names

- Analytical
- Stable
- King/Queen
- Lion

Overall Body Shape/Range of Motion/Energy/Locations of Tension

The Methodical Body Shape

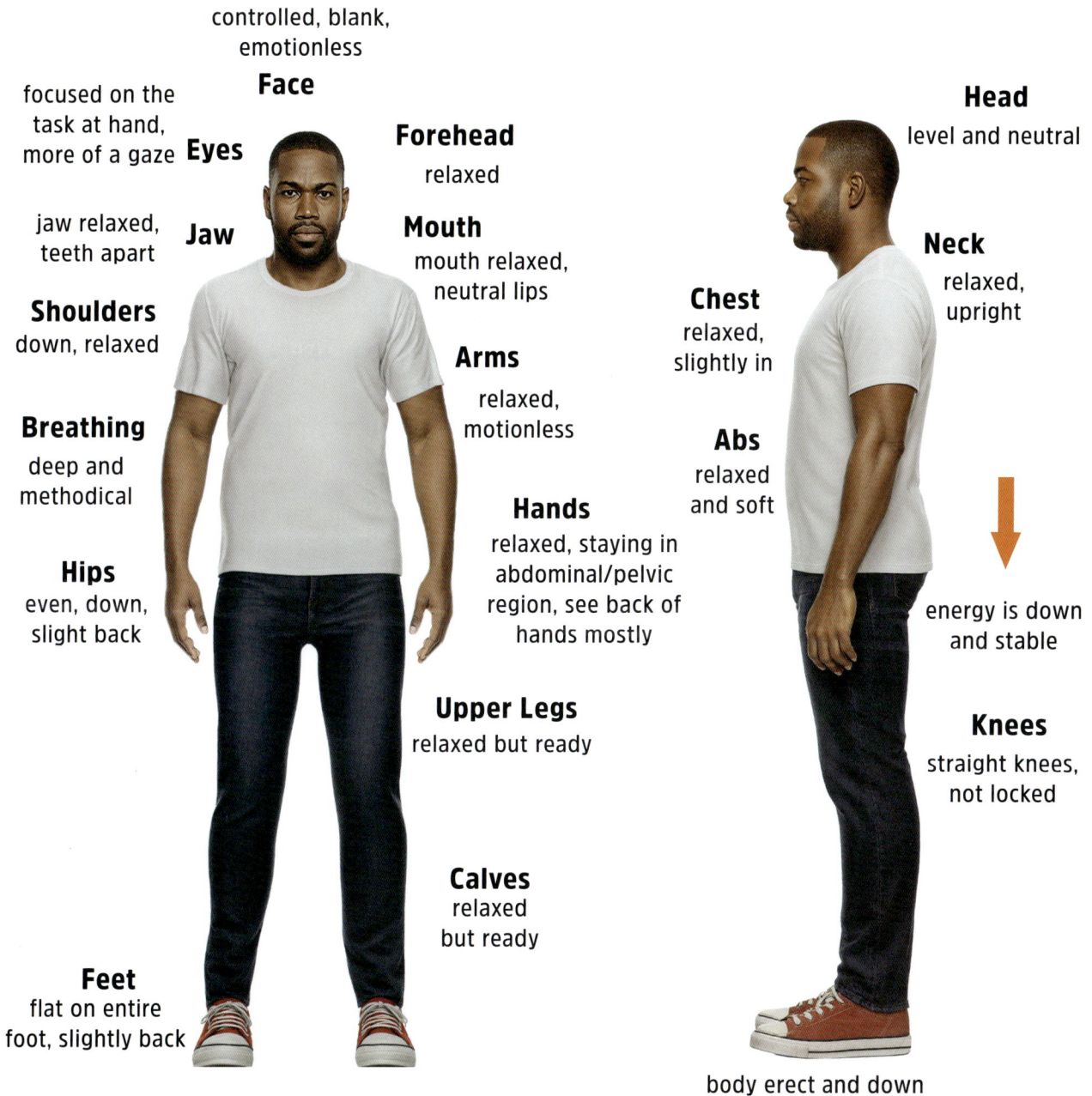

Face
controlled, blank, emotionless

Eyes
focused on the task at hand, more of a gaze

Forehead
relaxed

Jaw
jaw relaxed, teeth apart

Mouth
mouth relaxed, neutral lips

Shoulders
down, relaxed

Arms
relaxed, motionless

Breathing
deep and methodical

Hands
relaxed, staying in abdominal/pelvic region, see back of hands mostly

Hips
even, down, slight back

Upper Legs
relaxed but ready

Calves
relaxed but ready

Feet
flat on entire foot, slightly back

Head
level and neutral

Neck
relaxed, upright

Chest
relaxed, slightly in

Abs
relaxed and soft

energy is down and stable

Knees
straight knees, not locked

body erect and down

Additional Behaviors/Markers of the Methodical Body Shape

Facial Expression: The face of the methodical body shape is, for the most part, relaxed and without expression. The forehead is relaxed, without tension, as are the cheeks. The jaw is hanging and the teeth apart.

Body Posture/Energy: The body is "down" and slightly "back." Energy is methodical and on the slower side.

Range/Speed of Motion/Walking: Body movement is methodical and, more often than not, minimized. Walking is slow and straight.

Hands: This is the least likely of all four shapes to use the hands. When a person with this body type does use his or her hands, these are likely going to be minimal gestures in the lower abdomen region, and likely only the tips of the fingers and back of the hands will show. More indirect movement than direct.

Eyes: Are relaxed and open to, but not connecting with, others. This person is slowly scanning the horizon for data and information.

Voice: This is the most monotone in speech patterns of all the body shapes.
> Pace of Voice: slower pace, minimal inflection
> Volume: on the more quiet side, and unlikely to use volume to make a point
> Firmness: more on the soft side, not firm; rather static

Speaking: Not opinionated, but rather, when speaking, this person tends to share data and focuses on the task.

Word Usage: More gray and non-committal words; thinking-over-feeling words. Examples: "maybe," "at this time," "if possible," "the data says," "it would seem to me."

Speech: Subjects, Inflections, Descriptives:
> The subject of speech: task, process
> Inflection: little noticeable inflection
> Descriptives: facts, data

Time, Problem-Solve, 5W+H:
> Relation to Time: past-oriented; not necessarily affected by time; time is another variable; not time sensitive
> Problem-Solve: extremely linear and employing logical problem-solving through using tried and true methods
> 5 W+H: how

Humor, Clothing:

Humor: The least likely of all the body shapes to use humor; when this person does use, it is likely to be a dry humor, and many times the humor will not be seen as funny by others.

Clothing: The least fashion-conscious of all four shapes. Clothing is likely to be functional with the use of, even, drab colors. This person does follow organizational dress code as much as following his or her own personal uniform dress code.

The *Liquid Accordion* in Action « « « « « « «

The Methodical Body Shape: Famous People and Characters

Famous people with the methodical body shape are not likely to be front and center; in fact, they possess the body shape most likely to be in the background. They come across as more stoic, as not likely to be open and personal with others.

Famous People

Barack Obama	Meryl Streep
Harrison Ford	George Strait

Characters

Jerry Seinfeld (*Seinfeld*)	Mr. Spock (*Star Trek*)
Lisa Simpson (*The Simpsons*)	Mr. Data (*Star Trek*)
Mo (*Yellowstone*)	

Look to the Hands

"Hands have their own language."
Simon Van Booy[26]

When in doubt, when you are attempting to ascertain the basic body shape, a great place to observe is the hands. A way to think about it is that, as humans, one of the most likely places we take action is with our hands. From typing to eating to writing to scratching to covering a sneeze, we use our hands often. When we are talking, we also use our hands, and how we use our hands gives others a clue to our body shape. With each of the body shapes, you will likely see:

The Results Body Shape

- The hands will stay in the core of the body, specifically from the chest down to the navel, and close in. Overall, a very efficient use of the hands.

- When the person is using the hands to make a point, you will likely see the ends of the fingertips pointed forward, and hand gestures going forward and back.

- You will likely see the backs of the hands; you will be less likely to see the palms of the hands.

- Many times, you will see an index finger point.

- You may see both hands making a point.
- The hands be will used to make points; therefore, there will be times when the hands are not in use.
- The hands may be engaged in a task such as typing or writing as the person is talking.

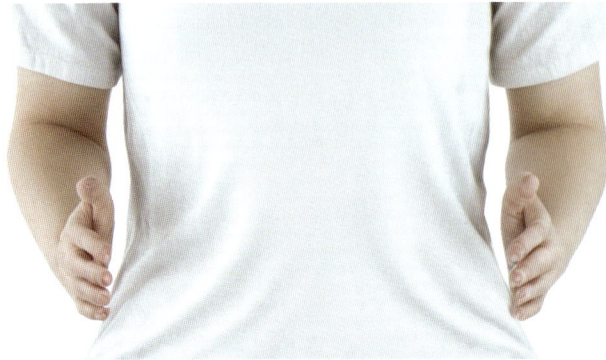

What you will not likely see:

- the palms of the hands
- the hands waving frantically outside the body
- the hands moving at all times

The Spontaneous Body Shape

- lots of hand movement
- lots of hand movement outside the core area of the body, including:
    - fist bumps
    - high-fives

- claps
- connecting with other bodies: touching, shaking hands, fist bumps
- palms and backs of the hands
- a correlation between the speaker's energy and their hand use—the more worked up they are, the more likely you will see their hands in motion
- both pointed and relaxed use of hands

What you will likely not see:

- limited use of the hands
- use of the hands only in the core of the body
- hands clasped and controlled

The Amiable Body Shape

- limited use of the hands
- hand use will be outside the core of the body but not to the extent of the spontaneous body
- When the hands are used, you will see:
    - flowing, relaxed, soft hands
    - palms of the hands
    - soft touch toward others (to connect)

What you will not likely see:

- overuse of the hands
- pointed gestures
- extreme gestures
- fists or aggressive use of the hands

The Methodical Body Shape

- the least amount of hand use when in conversation with others

- the hands will be limited to the core of the body and rarely leave the body area

- the backs of the hands and fingertips

- slower, more methodical use of the hands

What you will not likely see:

- large amounts of hand use

- palms of the hands

- hand use outside the core of the body

- fast movements with the hands

And there you have it. When in doubt, look to the hands!

The Fifth Body Shape: Center and Centeredness

"The key to good technique is to keep your hands, feet, and hips straight and centered. If you are centered, you can move freely."
Morihei Ueshiba[27]

Having just explored what we call the four basic body shapes, let's now explore a fifth body shape. First, though, we want to set up this concept. At any given time, as human beings, we are the liquid accordion that we are in that moment. We might be the results body shape, or the spontaneous body shape, or some other shape. In whatever shape we are in, we see the world through that perspective in that moment. For instance, if you are in the results body shape, you may be so focused on getting to the desired outcome you are seeking that you do not see or hear the conversations around you sharing that the direction you are heading is going to hit a brick wall! You are so focused that, literally, your hearing is tuned only to the sounds that address your task at hand, not any others. Your eyes may only be focused on the task at hand; you are unable to see other data. Your body may be leaning so forward that it cannot stop going in that direction. You are the body shape you are in.

In the moment that we are in a shape, we are, of course, not in any other shape. We have a shape, and we also have what we call an un-shape. Our un-shape is all the ways of being that we cannot access in that moment because we are in our shape. For instance, if in this moment I am in a methodical body shape, I cannot see possibilities in the other body shapes because my current body shape does not see the world the way an amiable or results body shape does.

How would we, then, be in a shape that allows us to see more possibilities? The shape that we are seeking is what we call the fifth basic body shape: *center or centeredness*. It is in center or centeredness that we can observe our shape/observer. In a sense, what we are doing is observing our observer. By doing this we can choose a shape/observer that will allow us to best show up to a situation. If we observe our observer from a shape such as an amiable shape or the methodical shape, we will likely only be able to see the world as that shape sees the world. It is from center, or centeredness, that we can see greater possibilities that are not shaded by the current shape we are in. In center we are not influenced by our stories, our moods/emotions, or even our body shape. Here are some key points to further explain center and centeredness.

Key Points About Center and Centering

Centering = choice

The idea is that if we are truly centered, we have choice. By being in center we have a choice of the moods/emotions we live in; we have a choice in how we show up in our bodies. In center we have the ability to choose an observer/shape that will help us create the future we desire to create. The more we practice and experience center, the more we can operate from that position, and the more we have choice.

Center does not mean mastery of other shapes

Just because we center and practice centering does not mean we have the ability to necessarily access and show up in a desired shape. If we desire to be more resolute in a situation, and we assess while in center that resolute is the shape that will serve us in this situation, it does not mean that we will be proficient, or even able to access, the desired shape or observer. The other shapes, just like center, must be practiced. The practice of center, though, allows us to access and practice the other shapes more readily, as we are in choice mode when we operate from center.

Center does not equal comfort

A common misconception when one starts centering practices is to equate center as where the practitioner feels "comfortable." In center the idea is that the practitioner is in a place of choice. If the practitioner has been in a body shape in the past which they have practiced, they might easily confuse the comfort of their shape to being in center. In fact, being in center, or centered, *may feel quite foreign and even uncomfortable.* For instance, if one spends a large amount of time in the spontaneous body shape, being centered my feel dull and boring, and the body may not know how to actually be still in the moment. This is why center is a shape that must be practiced.

Center requires practice

Repeating: center is a practice. Whatever your body shape, whatever your coachee's body shape, you both have been practicing it. Anything in life that we are good at, we have practiced. Can you write? Can you type? Can you read? The answer to all three of those questions is likely yes. How did you get good at them? You practiced. So if you want to be able to operate from center, you must practice being in center. The good news is that you must practice something, so why not start practicing center more?

Center is an assessment

Center is an assessment. That's right: an opinion or judgment. It is not an assertion, something which can be proven against a standard. Think about it: how will you know you are centered? Against what standard will you assess that you are centered? It is likely if you tried to ground your assessment, you will likely use another assessment to do so. It is likely that if you asked one hundred centering gurus what they assess center is, you would likely get many different forms or variations of a few definitions, but there would not actually be any way to prove you are centered. Also, we can only see the world as our bodies allow us to see the world (our historical discourse), and we cannot see what we have never seen or experienced. In this moment I may assess that I am centered, but tomorrow I may see centered from a different assessment and now have a different view of what center is. We can only know what we assess in a moment.

Bottom line: it is impossible to be truly centered in our bodies, but we can strive for this position.

Center is not a place we seek to always be in

If one were to always be centered, one could not take action. Think about it. Say I am sitting in what I assess to be a centered state. At some point I would need to take an action (go to the bathroom, eat, stand up, etc.), and to do that I will need a new shape to take that action. Because of this, center is not a place to live in but rather can serve us as a place to be in choice to take action. Once we are in a different shape, and take that action, we leave center. The real practice, then, becomes how quickly I can get back to center. It is from center that I can choose how to show up in a situation because I have to take action from another body disposition (resolute, spontaneous, amiable, methodical, or some melded version of these).

So what, then, is center? Let's look at it from an ontological and somatic perspective.

An Ontological Definition of Center

The simple ontological definition of center is the following.

From a body perspective, it is the *literal center of gravity,* which, tied to the martial arts traditions, is the *dan tien,* which is located approximately two-finger-widths below the belly button centered in the body. If one is centered in the body, then the body will be able to move in any direction with minimal effort. It is the axis of our length, our width, and our depth. When someone operates from their *dan tien,* they are operating from center. A way to envision this is to think of a ball sitting on a level tabletop in a two-dimensional space. The ball is not the center; the tabletop, due to its being level, represents center. If the table were to tilt in any direction, the ball would roll in that direction, and one would have to exert energy to keep the ball in center. Imagine this principle, now, in three dimensions. The ball, if the dimensions are centered, would find an equilibrium where the table would not have to hold it up. *This* is center.

From an emotional perspective, center is the state of acceptance. In acceptance there is not a predisposition to take any action; there is acceptance of what is. From this acceptance the observer can then have a choice of what actions to take. To be in any other mood/emotion means to be in that predisposition to take corresponding action.

From a linguistic perspective, center is silence. In silence we do not have a story, which is based on assessments, which create moods/emotions. It is in silence that one

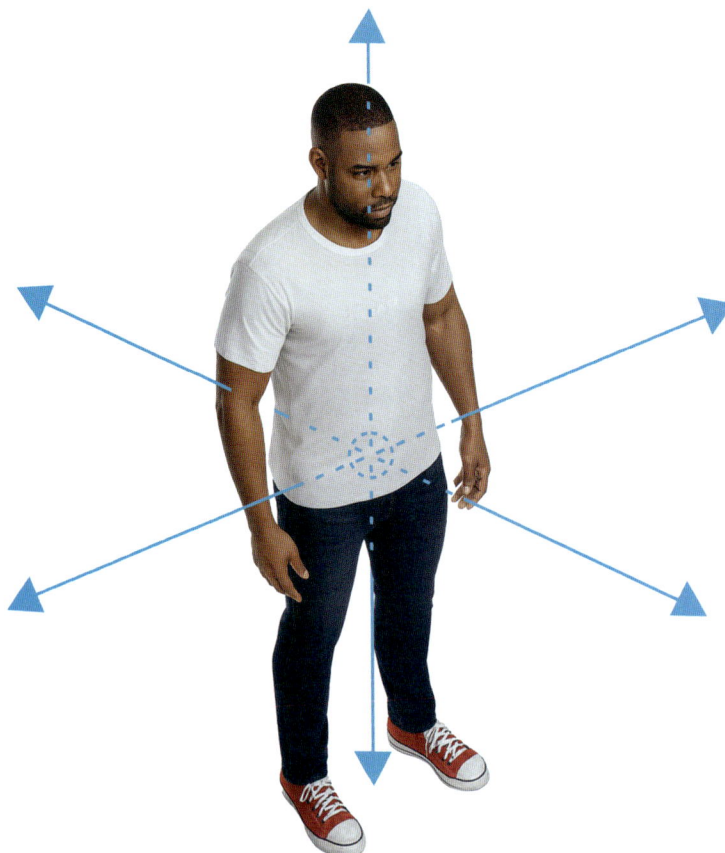

can choose an observer that aligns with what we care about. The challenge with silence, though, is that we as humans are rarely silent, except in a few instances on a daily basis or in a meditative state. Also, the moment that we begin to develop thoughts, we start to be off center . . .

In short, center is a tough place to find.

A Somatic Definition of Center

If we look at center from a solely somatic perspective, we would say that there are three dimensions: our length (from the bottom of our feet to the top of our head), our width (from the side of the body to the other opposing side), and our depth (from the front edge of our body to the back edge of the body). If these three dimensions are to intersect, the intersection is the place of center.

Although this may make sense, where it really shows up is when we are truly centered. If you have met someone who is extremely resolute, for instance, you will see that their body is leaning forward and their upper body and head leaning out/forward—so they are not centered. It is from a somatic place of center that we are in choice, and our body must represent this.

The *Liquid Accordion* in Action « « « « « « «

Even More of the Body in Language

We can use:
• elbow grease

Or we can . . .
• keep a cool head

We can put:
• muscle behind a task
• our back into something

We can keep:
• our eye on the ball
• our lips sealed

We can be:
• headstrong
• cocky

NINETEEN

The Body of Moods:
The Eight Basic Moods

"The right conversation in the wrong mood is the wrong conversation."
Julio Olalla[28]

We are human, we have a body, and we are, as humans, emotional beings. Where many are blind is that *moods/emotions live in and are created by the body*. Without our bodies we would not be able to have moods/emotions; we would not be human. As we humans navigate our world on a daily basis, we come across literally millions of data points. Whether we are aware of them or not, our liquid accordion—through its millions of sensors—notices things like temperature, visuals, pressures on our body, smells, sounds, and so on. We need some way to make sense of all the data, and the way we do it as humans is through moods/emotions. Moods/emotions are a *predisposition to action*. That is, they tell us what in our world is important and what in our world needs us to take action. Our body's shape causes our moods/emotions to change and our moods/emotions cause our body's shape to change as we navigate the world. This is the Liquid Accordion in action.

In his foundational work on ontological coaching, *Coaching to the Human Soul, Volume II,* Alan Sieler explores and brings together the idea that we as humans have several basic moods we experience in life. We will not try and rehash what is covered in the linguistic and emotional realm; rather, in our case, we will focus on the somatic aspects of each of the moods/emotions.

Eight Basic Moods

Acceptance

- **How the Mood/Emotion is Created:** accepting what is/accepting facticity

- **The Linguistic Assessments We Are Making Which Frame How We See the World:** "I accept what has happened. I may not like it, and it may not be what I desire, but I accept that this is reality."

- **Behavioral Disposition:** to take action in the realm of what is

- **How the Mood/Emotion Manifests in the Body:** Acceptance shows up somatically as a lack of somatic tension around what we accept. The body is open and relaxed and ready to move and take action in the current reality.

Resentment

- **How the Mood/Emotion is Created:** not accepting what is; not accepting facticity

- **The Linguistic Assessments We Are Making Which Frame How We See the World:** "This is not fair . . . this was done to me . . . they did it to me"

- **Behavioral Disposition:** to strike back or get even, to make those "who did it pay"

- **How the Mood/Emotion Manifests in the Body:** Resentment shows up in the body as tension and tightness. It can be prevalent in the pivot points (we'll unpack that term fully in the next chapter): the eyes, jaw, hands, and feet. It can also show up as tension in the neck and shoulders; also, in the face and lower back, and throughout the body.

Ambition

- **How the Mood/Emotion is Created:** accepting possibility

- **The Linguistic Assessments We Are Making Which Frame How We See the World:** "There are possibilities in my world, and I see and have actions to take."

- **Behavioral Disposition:** to take action in the realm of current and future possibilities

- **How the Mood/Emotion Manifests in the Body:** Ambition shows up in the body as the chest expansive and open. The head is up and scanning the horizon; the body is erect and upright. The arms and legs are a bit forward, ready for taking action. The arms can also be on the hips. In the body of ambition, all the vital organs (face, heart, lungs, internal organs, and genitals) are open and exposed to the world, but since this is a way of being that expresses belief in the ability to take action, there is a confidence to deal with any potential dangers. There is a light tension on the body, a slight armor to face the world. The body of ambition shows up as the archetype of Superman or Wonder Woman.

Resignation

- **How the Mood/Emotion is Created:** not accepting possibility

- **The Linguistic Assessments We Are Making Which Frame How We See the World:** a rational excuse of why things cannot change, a declaration that "change is not possible"

- **Behavioral Disposition:** to not take an action, except possibly to remain in the status quo and not change

- **How the Mood/Emotion Manifests in the Body:** Resignation shows up in the body as an overall slumped and downward-focused body. The head then tends to be looking down, which limits the ability to see other avenues. There is a heaviness to the body that makes taking action more difficult. There is a "sigh" of resignation and heaviness in the voice.

Wonder

- **How the Mood/Emotion is Created:** accepting of the unknown or uncertainty

- **The Linguistic Assessments We Are Making Which Frame How We See the World:** there is an unknown which "I desire to explore and learn about"

- **Behavioral Disposition:** An openness and curiosity to explore the unknown or uncertainty. There is not a need for certainty.

- **How the Mood/Emotion Manifests in the Body:** There is a lightness and curiosity in the body. The head is up, the eyes are wide and open to moving. There is an energy in the body to take action in any direction. The body is relaxed, but at the same time there is an energy to move. The arms are open, wide, and the palms are open and visible. The legs are a bit on the toes, the body slightly forward. Think of a kid at an amusement park for the first time.

Anxiety

- **How the Mood/Emotion is Created:** not accepting the unknown or uncertainty

- **The Linguistic Assessments We Are Making Which Frame How We See the World:** "The world is a dangerous place and I cannot deal with it. I might be hurt and cannot navigate this unknown."

- **Behavioral Disposition:** to protect and withdraw the body to a place of safety, to do whatever will protect me

- **How the Mood/Emotion Manifests in the Body:** In anxiety the body has a desire to shrink and not be prominent. The move is to shrink toward the fetal position, to protect the vital organs. The chest concaves in and the arms are moving inward to shield the body. While this is happening, the eyes and ears are hyper-alert, looking for data to deal with the uncertainty. There is an overall uneasiness in the body.

Sadness

- **How the Mood/Emotion is Created:** accepting the plain fact of loss

- **The Linguistic Assessments We Are Making Which Frame How We See the World:** "I have lost something I care about. Although I acknowledge that something I care about is lost forever, I am missing that, and longing for it."

- **Behavioral Disposition:** As we deal with sadness, we spend less energy looking back at what we lost and start to look more toward the present and the future. Still, though, we have periods where we are focused on what we have lost.

- **How the Mood/Emotion Manifests in the Body:** Eyes are dulled and have a general diminished aspect to the body. The energy is a bit hindered and limited at times as the body moves forward. There is a lack of crispness in movements and actions.

Grieving

- **How the Mood/Emotion is Created:** not accepting the sheer fact of loss

- **The Linguistic Assessments We Are Making Which Frame How We See the World:** "I do not accept this loss, and I want to have the world the way it was before the loss."

- **Behavioral Disposition:** To spend our time, energy, and focus on the loss and making sense of the loss; at the same time, not wanting to accept that it has happened

- **How the Mood/Emotion Manifests in the Body:** A heaviness in the body, as if there is a huge weight, or burden, weighing down the body. The eyes do not look up and engage, but rather are cast down and inward-focused. The arms and legs are labored to move and lift. There can also be writhing and shifting in the body as it processes the grief.

TWENTY

The Four Pivot Points

"Since we cannot change reality, let us change the eyes which see reality."
Nikos Kazantzakis[29]

What is a pivot point? We can explore dictionaries for various definitions. From the aspect of coaching in, with, and through the body, two stand out:

1) *A thing or factor which has a major function, role, or effect;*

and

2) *The act of turning on a pivot*[30]

Are there key pivot points, or *locations in the body,* on which *change, and awareness, will have a disproportional effect on the person changing?* These are places where, if they are clear, the coach—while coaching, in, with and through the body—would have disproportionate effect on change for the individual. There are four places for the coach to explore in the coachee which will help the coachee pivot. They are, in no order of importance: the eyes, jaw, hands, and feet. We start with the eyes.

The Eyes

Try this exercise: Right now, relax your eyes. Keep your eyes open, but relax them. Allow your gaze to relax to the point that you are not focusing on anything in your field of view. Does your body match your eyes? My assessment is that it will. Now, focus your eyes on an object. Really see the object. Look at the object as if you are burning a hole in the object with your eyes. What happens to your body when you do this?

It has been said that the eyes are the window to the soul. They are also a key in focusing the body. As we navigate a typical day, there are literally millions of data points coming at us throughout that day. And as we navigate the world, we need a quick way to take in the much of the data. An effective tool to do that is with the eyes. They see things all around us, both straight ahead and in our periphery. The shape of the eyes in the moment determines what we see. Are our eyes focused? Are they relaxed? Are they up? Are they down? It is the shape, in the moment, that we can then coach to.

Helping the coachee to "see" something differently is shifting the observer. If someone is laser-like in their focus they will see only what they focus on. If, however, we can help them relax their eyes and not be so focused, we can help them "see" something different.

Notice how, in the what/where of coaching in, with, and through the body section of this book, we see the eyes in all of the different body types:

- Chakra: the "third eye" or "brow chakra" is a standalone chakra

- Body armoring: the ocular band

- The four body dispositions: all look at how the eyes show up in eye contact

It is not a coincidence that all of the body methodologies touch on the eyes as they are such a critical and pivotal way to shift one's observer.

The Jaw

Another key somatic pivot point is the jaw.

Try this exercise: try to lift something quite heavy (don't overdo it; I do not want to have a bill for your hospital visit show up because you took me literally and tried to lift a small car!). Make the lift toward the edge of your safe capabilities of strength, and remember to lift beginning with the legs! Now, as you lift, what happens to your jaw? At some point your jaw will be clenched because, to lift without a clenched jaw would mean we are not lifting to our capacity. Think about what the jaw does to your face when you clench it. Clenching it allows all of the head and facial muscles to engage in the process of lifting, and this gives us more strength. (Also note that when we are growling or grunting, our jaw is clenched.)

Like most people who regularly visit the dentist, many of us have likely been told by our dentist that our teeth are wearing down from over-clenching. This is a way that we as humans deal with stress; we clench our jaws. But what happens when we relax our jaw? We experience very different emotions. The jaw is a pivot point of coaching in, with, and through the body.

Did you know that the strongest muscle in the body is the masseter, also known as the jawbone? It is even stronger in certain groups, such as politicians and social media influencers. It gets lots of use making promises and smiling for votes and likes.

The Hands

Think of any physical activity you do: driving, writing, typing, clapping, running, and many more. All of them involve the hands. Remember earlier in the book when we talked about standing up from a chair; what was the first thing we did? Almost all of those activities involve, and many begin with, the hands. If I want to write an email, one of the first things I do is start to move my hands up to the keyboard. Think about what happens when you do that, or really, when you take any action involving your hands. Not only are the muscles in your hands engaged, all of the muscles going from the tips of your fingers back to your core are engaged—all of them, on some level. Take it to extremes: what happens when someone is about to hit something with a clenched fist? The entire body is tense, and the entirety of the core is engaged. This is the power of pivot in the hands.

The Feet

Much like the hands, the feet are extreme points of the body and, when used, engage muscles all the way back to the core. Think about the simple act of standing erect. There is constant expansion/contraction of the muscles from the sole of the feet all the way up to the core. What happens when we start to walk forward? Our entire muscular system is engaged. The feet are another key pivot point in the body.

* **Note about people who do not have eyesight, or cannot use their jaw, hands, or feet:** there are still pivot points; this person cannot pivot on one or more of these four but will likely rely on other pivot points. For instance, someone who has limited or no eyesight would then likely have other senses (hearing, feel, touch, taste) heightened, and would therefore not pivot in the same way as someone who has those capabilities.

» PART 3

THE HOW OF COACHING IN, WITH, AND THROUGH THE BODY

. . . .

The How of Coaching In, With, and Through the Body

We have explored the why and the what/where of coaching in, with, and through the body. We now turn to what, for many coaches, is the missing piece: that is *how* to coach in, with, and through the body. This part of the book will have very specific methods—and in some cases, even scripts—of how to do this. The goal is to set the coach up with ways to somatically coach that have been proven and are adaptable to specific coaching situations.

The section begins with an often-overlooked body in coaching: the body of the coach. We will explore practices such as:

- center in the body of the coach

- the four body shapes in the coach

- "down and back" as a coach

- the somatic tuning fork

- the moods and emotions of the coach

This part of this section will then set up the somatic arc of coaching for reference for the coach.

The next part of this third section then explores somatic coaching tools to coach the coachee. These include:

- breathing techniques for the coachee

- centering techniques for the coachee

- the Scanner Technique, a well-proven method to coach with (this will include a script for the coach to start with)

- somatic role-playing

- coaching to the four body shapes

- Breathe to Blend, a somatic technique to help coachees engage in conversation with others when they are in a triggered state

- expand/contract

- coaching to the four pivot points

- coaching to chakras/body armoring

- a list of somatic practices and disciplines

- references

- glossary

- somatic/ontological/generative learning organizations

Let's get going with coaching in, with, and through the body . . .

TWENTY-
ONE

Foundations of How to Coach In, With, and Through the Body

"The human body is the best picture of the human soul."
Ludwig Wittgenstein[31]

We have explored the why of coaching in, with, and through the body. We have looked at the what and where of this coaching. Now we will explore the how to coach in, with, and through the body. First, though, a few key points to remember, and while we're at it, let's set the stage for a context of coaching in, with, and through the body.

Get Used to Practicing (the P in SELPH)

As you start your journey of coaching in, with, and through the body, it is critical that you start with the idea that somatics is not about being perfect (nor is life for that matter!). As a coach, practice is a close friend of learning and competence. One of my favorite experiences with Julio Ollalo, the founder of ontological coaching, was when I once watched him interact with a participant in a program. There was a person in the audience who said, "Oh, Julio, I would love to do what you do." Julio, being Julio, said with a playful grin, "It is quite simple, actually. You simply have the same conversation every day for 30 years!" If we as coaches want to find mastery with any aspect of coaching in, with, and through the body, we must put in the practice. This book, and the knowledge gained from the practices in this book, are just a start. As the title suggests, a primer is "a small introductory book on a subject." Start here, but do not end here. To learn more about somatics, one must practice and make practice *an everyday practice.*

Allow Space to Be a Beginner

Although it may seem a bit contradictory at first, being a beginner, and putting in lots of practice, go hand in hand. As you are starting on this journey to learn about coaching in, with, and through the body, a great place to start is as a beginner. Some aspects of a beginner:

- Declare you do not know something about the subject! Good news: it is likely you did this when you bought this book, so you have one down . . .

- You are willing to find and listen to a coach you trust and allow that coach to coach you in that domain. (Two for two! That is, if you trust me, the author; if not, you might want to coach yourself about being coachable. But I am going to bet you are at least a bit coachable, and you are trusting the author if you have made it this far.)

- You follow the instructions of the coach. You will see in the following techniques that it is recommended you follow the scripts and actions, initially, to a tee. There is a method to the madness: trust in the learning and in the coach.

- You are coachable. Are you? It is the million-dollar question. If you are, you might be able to tap into the wisdom of the many wise and embodied teachers who have made this book a reality.

One last thought about being a beginner. A question for you as you explore: how does being a beginner show up for you in your body? If you are unaware, this is not a problem; many of the exercises that follow will reveal that to you as you head down this path. If you are aware of how it shows up for you, I would challenge you to really practice the following techniques with the body of a beginner.

You Do Not Have to Be an Expert to Coach In, With, and Through The Body

A great aspect of coaching in, with, and through the body is that you do not have to "get it right" to help the coachee create more powerful awareness in the coaching journey. Two key points help us explore this further.

Coaching In, With, and Through the Body Is Not an Exact Science

Each human being is unique, obviously, and therefore coaching in, with, and through the body will be unique with each coachee. We are not saying that in coaching in, with, and

Coaching Tips

Let's provide some basic tips on being a beginner.

If you are struggling to be a beginner, see if you can tap any of the following emotions:

- curiosity
- lightness
- playfulness
- awe
- wonder

What body would you have to be in to tap into any of the above emotions?

Where would your body be expanding? Where would it be contracting?

What would your story be when you are a beginner?

through the body that A + B = C every time. Rather, we are aware that many times when we see A and B, we will likely see C. But not every time, and nor is our goal to turn this into a formula. Allow the beauty, and mystery, to show up in your coaching, and be open to not seeing C if you see A and B.

The Coachee Is the Most Qualified Subject Matter Expert for Their Body (Whether They Know It or Not)

As you are coaching someone in, with, and through their body, know that they are the one with direct access to their body. Now, direct access does not mean they are aware of their body, nor does it mean they can access their body. The good news is that the coach, with practice and awareness themselves, can help the coachee become more aware of his or her body. Through practice and exploration the coachee can tap the wisdom and guidance that their body provides. Allow mystery to be an ally of the coach and coachee in this exploration.

The Coachee's Lack of Awareness in Their Body Might Be the Breakdown They Are Seeking

It is not uncommon to be coaching someone in the body who is disconnected from their body and, in the initial coaching conversations, this becomes quite apparent. The beautiful thing is that through coaching in, with, and through the body the coach can help open up the coachee's body as a place of knowledge and wisdom, and this allows the coachee to discover the path forward in themselves.

Trust Your Body in the Process

A large part of being a somatic and ontological coach is to trust your body. Your body has a wisdom and an understanding that your conscious thought may not be able to understand or fully translate into language. As you are coaching others, allow your body to inform you where to go with the coaching conversations. Listen to intuitions, feelings, and inklings that reside in your body to inform you and your coaching conversations. As we will explore just a bit later, this is a key aspect of coaching in, with, and through the body.

Do Not Get Trapped in Your Body and Your Story

A challenge you may face when coaching others is that your body shows up as it has habitually shown up in the past. Because of this, when the coachee is experiencing deep emotional/somatic upheaval or breakdowns, it is likely your body will want to go where it is most comfortable. Here's an example: when a coachee is experiencing extreme sadness and is crying, the coach's conditioned tendencies might be to soothe and comfort the coachee in the sadness. This is not coaching, but rather is the coach dealing with their own issues. This is not to say the coach cannot show empathy; rather, the goal of the coach is to build the container for the coachee to be in their breakdown. If the coach is wrestling with his or her own emotions around the coachee's breakdown, they cannot serve the coachee. This is why it is critical to coach from center and in a place where we, the coaches, can best show up.

Coach in the Body, Not in the Story

It is always the body . . . In the end, we can talk about the body, but we must always practice *in* the body to learn about the body. The only way to master anything is to have it be embodied. Therefore, when you are coaching others about the body, you must take them *to* their body and they must practice *in* the body. Instead of talking about emotions, have the coachee be in their body and *experience* the emotion. In my practices as a mentor/coach I cannot tell you how many times the coach had the coachee talk about their body as if they were describing the landscape of the moon. Instead, have the coachee actually *feel* how and where the emotion is living and emanating from.

Let's start with a body you may or may not be aware of . . . *yours*!

The Body of a Coach:
Coaching from Center

"Stay centered, do not overstretch, extend from your center, return to your center."
Buddha[32]

As we shift to the how of coaching in, with, and through the body, we need to be aware that in any coaching conversation, from a somatic perspective, there are at least two bodies present: the body of the coachee(s) and the body of the coach. We will start with the body you will be getting to know quite well, if you have not already, and that is the body of the coach, i.e., you! Regardless of the type of coaching you do, your body will always be present in the coaching conversation, so we will start there.

Every aspect of this book so far, and the rest of the book, for that matter, applies to your body, just as it does the body of the coachee. I would go so far as to make the declaration that the more you, as a coach, understand, live, feel, and inhabit your body, the more your abilities as a coach will grow and flourish.

Your ability to coach yourself in, with, and through the body will determine how well you can coach others in, with, and through their bodies.

A key point is this: as you are coaching, it is the *listening* in, with, and through your body that will allow you to start to have the "Jedi" wisdom that masterful coaches seem to have. It is in the listening that the body allows things such as intuition and instincts to come alive. Listen in, with, and through your body as a coach to help the coachee listen in, with, and through their body.

The goal of your somatic practices as a coach is to bring your most powerful somatic self to each and every coaching conversation. To do this you will have to take your body from "in the way"—possibly numb, triggered, or off-center—to a place where your observer is integrated, and your body is the tool to help you as a coach help your coachee unlock his or her potential.

Think of what would be your best body as a coach. What would it be like? What would its shape be? How would you create a body that, instead of hindering your abilities as a coach, actually allowed all of your abilities as a coach to come forward and come alive?

Can you get your body to a place of curiosity, flexibility, openness, and playfulness to coach others? To do that, I want to share several ways to explore your body as a coach.

Four Coach Bodies

- the centered body to leverage the four basic body shapes

- the "down and back" body

- the somatic tuning fork

- the powerful moods body

Let's begin to break down these four coaching bodies.

TWENTY-THREE

The Need for Center as a Coach

"He who conquers himself is the mightiest warrior."
Confucius

So you are a coach and you enter a coaching session with a coachee. As you enter a conversation, you as a coach are somehow triggered by the conversation. You are now struggling with your observer when you are attempting to support the coachee's observer. How or why does this happen? You as a coach can and will get triggered, or off center, with the coachee and will find that your ability to coach others is not effective unless you have the ability to coach yourself.

So what can cause you, as a coach, to get triggered in the coaching session? You can get triggered by the coachee in three domains:

- their **shape** (body)

- their **story** (language)

- their **emotions** (moods/emotions)

Where have we seen this before? That's right: the coachee's BEL can, and will, influence your BEL—that is, if you allow it to. How then do masterful coaches (or leaders, or gurus, etc.) *not* allow the BEL of others to influence their BEL? They do it by being masterful at finding center, also known as being centered. This is the most basic practice of being a coach.

It is critical, then, that you coach from center, from a place where you are in choice of how to best serve the coachee and their needs. This allows you as the coach to blend with the coachee and meet them where *they* are—as opposed to where you are stuck. Your ability to dance (blend) with the coachee, wherever they are, is extremely important. Center allows the coach to hold a big space for the coachee to bring their challenges, their strong emotions, or their stories to the conversation without the coach's emotions getting in the way. If you can coach from center, you can choose which observer will best serve the coachee. This is where we begin our *how* of coaching in, with, and through the body.

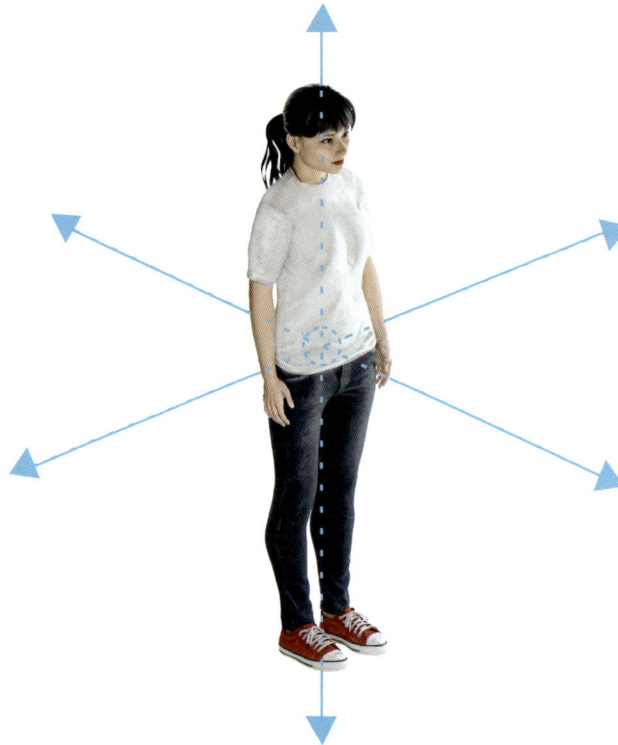

>> >> >> >> >> >> >> >> >> >>   **The *Liquid Accordion* in Action**

Others in 'The Body in Language'

Others can:

- give us an evil stare
- keep an eye on us
- stick their nose in our business
- pay lip service
- give us a slap on the wrist
- give us a hand
- get off our backs
- give us a pat on the back

- be a pain in the ass
- pull our leg
- foot the bill
- make our blood boil
- be flesh and blood
- stab us in the back
- turn their back on us
- breathe down our necks

TWENTY- FOUR

Coaching from the Four Body Shapes

"We only believe in those thoughts which have been conceived, not in the brain, but in the whole body."
William B. Yeats[33]

If we are coaching from center, we are in choice. We are in choice on how we can best serve the coachee in the moment. To do this we must be able to access a somatic observer of our own, and this then serves what we assess that the situation calls for. Which one we choose will be dependent on the situation and shape of the coachee. Our goal here is not to be formulaic, but rather to show the manifold options available to the coach in any given situation. Therefore, what you will see below is how each of the four body shapes may serve the coach and how each of the body dispositions may not serve the coach. In the end, it is the acquired wisdom of your observer that allows the body disposition to show up in shapes which best serve the coachee. This a good place to start.

Results Body

Serves:

Taking action

Cutting through story and getting to breakdown

Initiating difficult conversations

Keeping conversations on time

Keeping conversations on topic

Focus on completion

Does not serve:

Can lead to win/lose mentality

Can lead to all/nothing mentality

Missed listening

Spontaneity

Lightness, playfulness

Limited emotional responses

The energy/body can be so forward that the coach is not in a place to listen

Spontaneous Body

Serves:

Playfulness in the moment

Lightheartedness

The ability to adapt to changes in emotions in the coachee

The ability to be more visionary and creative in the situation

Being in a "dance" with the coachee

Does not serve:

A lack of focus

A lack of attention to detail

Being so in the emotions that the emotions overpower being centered

Can be self-centered

Can tell personal stories that might not serve the coachee

Amiable Body

Serves:

Strong emotions of vulnerability

Intimacy

Trust

Slow and open pace of call

Lightness, playfulness

Does Not Serve:

Strong emotions, specifically of anger, rage, or other strong "negative" emotions

Conflict in the call

Difficult conversations

Interrupting to keep call on time or on topic

Methodical Body

Serves:

Removes chaos and uncertainty by staying stable and calm

Allows space for the coachee to share their stories and assessments

Allows for a deep dive into details

Allows for a slower pace

Does not serve:

Vulnerability

Need to get to finish of the call

Need to keep call on time or topic

Can get into weeds or too deep into a story

Down and Back

"The body says what words cannot."
Martha Graham[34]

The method of "Down and Back" is a way for the coach to show up as a powerful somatic container for the coachee to be supported in the coaching conversation. It is mostly about how the coach shows up in the call, creating a large "container" for the coachee to be with their breakdowns. The idea of a container is that the coach holds a space that is large enough for the coachee to bring their whole observer to the coaching conversation. This includes strong moods and emotions and stories that are holding back the coachee from creating a new future. To do this, it is critical for the coach to show up with energy and a way of being that is down (grounded, connected to the earth) and back (very present, and accepting of the coachee and their situation). To be "down and back," the coach can be standing or sitting. If the coach is sitting, it is critical they sit in a chair that is conducive to being down and back.

Here are the entities involved in down and back:

- **The chair:** Although it may sound a bit far out to investigate furniture in somatic coaching, hang with us as we explore the type of chair necessary for down and back. The chair needs to be quite sturdy and provide support for the coach. The chair can be comfortable, but it is critical that the chair have a seat which allows the coach's "seat" bones to be fully connected to the seat. It needs a back to the chair which is as close to vertical as possible so the coach can fully connect with the back of the chair and sit as vertical as possible. The chair should be at a height that allows the coach's feet to firmly connect with the ground and positions the coach's thigh bones parallel to the ground. Armrests allow the coach's arms to be supported so they are parallel with the thigh bones. This allows the coach to open his or her hands palms up.

- **The coach:** If the chair "fits" the coach nicely, it allows the coach to fully relax his or her body and allow the chair and gravity to do most of the work for the coach's liquid accordion to relax and be fully present with the coachee. As the coach sits with the coachee, arms are palms up or down, relaxing on the armrests, and the coach is operating from a relaxed, centered, somatic shape, open to the conversation. This, of course, is dependent on the coach's current shape, and with practice the down and back can be mastered.

- **"Holding a massive beach ball"**: If the coach shows up as down and back, this opens up a shape that will allow the coach to "hold the container" for the coachee and their breakdowns and stories. An analogy to demonstrate this is for the coach to be in a shape which would allow him or her to hold a very large beach ball—this represents the coachee's breakdown.

What Is a Breakdown?

The terms *break in transparency* and *breakdown* have specific meanings in the onto-logical coaching/somatic coaching disciplines. Here are a few details about each.

Break in transparency: something which causes us, as humans, to become aware of something that previously was transparent to us. A simple example is, as you are walking down the sidewalk, you see, ahead of you, a tree fall across the sidewalk about 50 feet straight ahead. Prior to the tree falling you were likely not even aware of it in your consciousness. As it falls, there is a break in this transparency. You are now aware of it. This, however, does not affect you as you are turning away from the tree to walk in another direction so you would not have to walk around or over the tree.

Breakdown: A breakdown is a break in transparency that causes one to have to take action. As in our previous example, the tree falling across the sidewalk is a breakdown for you because you need to walk on the sidewalk where the tree has fallen to get to your friend's house. Because of this breakdown, you are going to have to take action. You will have to cross to the other side of the street and then double back to get to your friend's house, or you might change your plans and not go to your friend's house. This break-down affects your future actions. This is relevant in coaching because the "breakdowns" a coachee brings to a coaching conversation are why they are seeking a coach—to help them become more powerful observers of their breakdowns, and to take more effective actions to navigate the breakdowns.

Because the coach's body is relaxed and open, and the chair and gravity are doing most of the work, the coach can sustain a deep and heavy conversation in a manner that allows the coachee to be with their breakdown and feel supported by the coach.

Coaching In, With, and
Through the Body in Action: Vanessa

Vanessa, a beginner coach, was getting frustrated with her coaching sessions. She found that she was especially getting frustrated with several of her clients because, as she shared in a mentoring coaching session, they were "never taking any action." She shared with her coach that she was passionate about her coaching and really wanted to help her coachees succeed. She said that what attracted her to coaching was the ability to help her clients live a "life well lived." As her mentor coach observed a recorded video session, it became obvious in the taped call that Vanessa was herself in a body of action, as evidenced by her sitting forward and being in action in her body. In the debrief, the coach offered Vanessa to sit down and back, as her mentor coach was doing at that time. At first Vanessa struggled to be down and back; it felt, she shared, as though she was falling backward. Her coach offered for her to keep with it in their call. Slowly, Vanessa eased into her chair and allowed the chair to hold her up and support her. What she began to see was that the call seemed to slow down and be more about learning than "getting somewhere." As the call ended, Vanessa committed to try the down and back in her next few coaching calls with her clients.

In their next mentoring session Vanessa showed up as a different coach. She shared that through being down and back she had a newfound ability to really listen to her coachees and be in a place of exploration with them. She shared that what was most interesting for her, though, was that as she showed up down and back with her clients, her own frustrations disappeared! This was because she was not living in a body that needed to take action.

The Somatic Tuning Fork

"I become like a tuning fork to the information that is coming through me;
in shamanism they call it being the 'hollow reed.'"
Tom Kenyon[35]

It is necessary to make a distinction about coaching in, with, and through the body. As the statement suggests, we coach in the body, we coach with the body, and we coach through the body. It is likely that as one hears this their thoughts of "in, with, and through the body" are about the coachee's body—and they are. They are also, though, and just as importantly, about the coach's body. A transformational/somatic/ontological coach coaches *in* their own body, *with* their own body, and *through* their own body. The body then becomes the tool of the transformational/somatic/ontological coach. This tool allows the coach to mirror the coachee in all three domains: body, moods/emotions, and language. The analogy we use for the body as a tool is what we call the somatic tuning fork.

In science a tuning fork allows one to create waves with the instrument by striking the fork on a single end in such a way that the two tines of the fork vibrate to a specific metronomic frequency, matching the frequency of a tune.

It is in the same way with the body in transformational/somatic/ontological coaching. It is the coach's body that is "listening" for the frequency of the coachee's body, their story, their emotions. As the coach's somatic tuning fork starts to resonate with the coachee's body, emotions, and story, the resonance allows the coach's body to inform them of the observer that the coachee is. By using the coach's own body as a tool to listen, the coach can access insights which can inform the coach of the entire observer of the coachee. The coach whose body is in "limbic and somatic resonance" with the coachee is, in essence, experiencing the world the coachee is feeling and experiencing. It is from this awareness that the coach accesses in his or her own body that the coach can then allow the questions and observations which they share with the coachee. The questions and observations come from the coach's being, from his or her deep listening, as opposed to only the intellectual domain.

>> >> >> >> >> >> >> >>   **The *Liquid Accordion* in Action**

Did you know that when we are born we have 300 bones? By the time we die, assuming we reach adulthood, that number has been reduced to only 206 bones! The liquid accordion is never staying still.

It is critical, though, that the coach listens extremely well to the coachee's story, emotions, and body but does *not get triggered* by the coachee's story, emotions, or body. To do this the somatic tuning fork of the coach resonates with the coachee's frequency, so to speak, but the coach does not take on the coachee's body, emotions, or story. The reason we then go "down and back" is that it is critical for the coach to coach from a body which is centered and stable—i.e., down and back—allowing their body to resonate with the coach's body. Again, the more this happens the more the coach can share questions and observations which are actually informed by the coachee, not just by the coach.

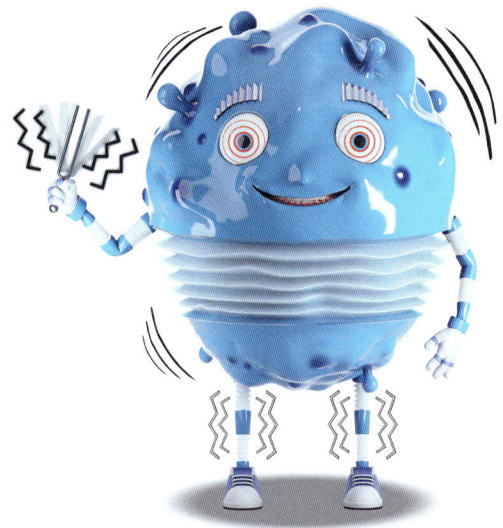

The somatic tuning fork, in essence, becomes about the coach trusting his or her own intuitions and somatic wisdom. This wisdom allows for powerful coaching in, with, and through the body.

TWENTY-SEVEN

The Moods/Emotions of Choice for a Coach

"Over the years our bodies become walking autobiographies that tell friends and strangers alike of the major and minor stresses of our lives."
Marilyn Ferguson[36]

As a coach, your emotions affect the coachee. Therefore, what if you were to choose some emotional states to operate from in a coaching conversation? There is not a set-in-stone or "perfect" emotional state, but rather this can become a practice for the coach in how to show up. Some powerful moods to show up in as a coach include the following.

Lightness: In lightness we are without the heavy burdens that can affect how we see the world. This can be a very effective emotional state for the coach as it keeps the heaviness of the coachee's situation with the coachee and not on the coach. Lightness shows up in the body in the following ways:

• There is an overall relaxing of the body and, with the body's energy, a moving up and out.

• There is a hint of a smile in the mouth.

• The pivot points (eyes, jaw, hands, and feet) are relaxed and open to moving.

Gentle Irreverence: Gentle irreverence allows us to be lighthearted and a bit playful in the face of heavy and serious situations. It is not about mocking or disregarding a serious topic but rather is about keeping a perspective of not being overwhelmed by the seriousness of the situation at hand. It allows the coach to offer a bit of lightheartedness to the coachee so they may see a glimpse of hope. Gentle irreverence shows up in the body in these ways:

- An overall lightness and playfulness in the body. This is a bit of excess energy looking for a place to go, a bit of a dance in the body.

- Energy is moving up and out, with an open and more expansive chest.

- A slight smile on the face, a comfortable laugh at the ready.

Curiosity: This is an emotional state that allows one to be seeking answers, but not in a "right" answer orientation. Instead, it is rather as a seeking of the truth, whatever that might be. Curiosity allows for movement forward so there is an energy in the body to move and explore. Here are some of the ways in which curiosity shows up in the body:

- The eyes are a bit more focused, looking for something the observer seeks, yet at the same time they are wide, allowing peripheries of the vision to reveal itself.

- The body is a bit forward, and there is a bit of energy seeking to take action.

- The feet are slightly on the balls of the feet, ready to move forward to where the learning resides.

The Somatic Arc of Coaching

"The body cannot lie. It is incapable of lying.
Only what comes out of the mouth can lie; the body never lies."
Stanley Keleman[37]

It is critical to understand the somatic arc of coaching when we are coaching others. Any successful coaching interaction will likely follow some arc, including the following.

Current Observer/Current Shape

We start with the coachee being a current observer. At any given point the coachee is in a somatic shape that, as we have previously explored, has a SELPH. The current observer has a history of practice that has led that person to the current shape of body, and moods/emotions, and also has a story of the situation.

Current Shape

(Current Observer)
SELPH
Length, Width,
Depth, Commitment

Trigger

At some point the coachee, who is navigating the world as the observer he or she is, experiences some form of trigger. The trigger can be from many things, such as another person, a conversation, a situation, or a familiar or even unfamiliar physical world. The trigger can be real, it can be perceived, it can be obvious, or it can be hidden. Whatever it is, the trigger causes in the current observer some emotional, linguistic, and somatic shift which is the observer's way of taking actions to deal with the trigger.

Historical Tendency

Whatever the trigger, the observer we are needs to take different actions. Therefore, a new somatic shape, a new emotional state, and a new story all combine to create what we call a historical tendency. Since we are historical beings, in the past we likely experienced a similar situation or trigger, which, because we are embodied, became part of our repertoire to deal with that and similar situations. The historical tendency, which is some combination of expansion/contraction of the liquid accordion that we all are, for all intents and purposes happens

Historical Tendency
New SELPH Length, Width, Depth, Commitment

instantaneously. The observer we are, in a sense, created a shortcut so that we navigate the world in a future state we will know and be familiar with. "If X, or something like X, happens, then we become observer Y to deal with it." (Go back to Chapter 5 dealing with the Embodied Pattern of the Liquid Accordion and Center for more information, or to review.) This literal historical tendency allows us to grow as humans and to develop the embodiment to navigate the complexities of life. The challenges, though, can be: 1) the historical tendency we have embodied over years of practice is no longer sufficient to deal with the trigger; 2) we experience a situation that, although our observer assesses it, is like another situation warranting the historical tendency. The new trigger is not likely to be served by the historical tendency.

Two Paths

The historical tendency we are unknowingly practicing can take one of two paths.

- If we allow our historical tendency to dictate the observer we are now in, we have now just practiced, and further embodied, that historical tendency, making it more likely to be how we navigate the situation in the future.

Or,

- We become aware of the breakdown and choose a different path. This new path creates a new somatic awareness, which, along with the accompanying story and emotional state, starts us on a new path. This somatic awareness can be brought to life through many different modalities such as:
  - coaching
  - a somatic practice
  - a new awareness of the breakdown

Regardless of how it is created, the new somatic awareness starts us on a new, different trajectory of learning and development of our observer.

Unbounded State

The unbounded state is a state in which a person's somatic shape leaves its old, historical tendency/shape and creates a new shape. The challenge/opportunity in the unbounded state is that the old shape, which is revealed to the observer as no longer serving him or her, is no longer a possibility. The new shape, though, has not developed or been revealed, so the body is literally in an unbounded state. The old is not possible, but the new is not yet evolved. One way that we as humans may navigate this is to find the quickest new way to be at the new shape so there is as little discomfort as possible.

Unbounded State
Old Shape is no longer viable, New Shape has yet to evolve

There is another possible way to navigate the unknown and unbounded state, and that is to *be in the uncomfortableness* and allow the new shape to start to reveal itself as the coachee engages in some sort of practice in the unbounded shape. This practice will allow the new, more effective shape to emerge.

Practice

It is in the practicing that the unbounded shape starts to morph into the new somatic shape. If the practice is allowed to evolve and be a regular practice, then the evolution of the new shape can be more powerful, opening up for the observer a shape that will truly serve him or her. What the practice is, and the length of time for each situation and individual, is different. The point is that to create/evolve into a new shape takes practice. (I think we heard that in a few other places in this book. Maybe there is a theme developing here . . .)

Practice

New Observer/New Somatic Shape

As the coachee practices, the new somatic shape will emerge, and with enough practice the coachee will evolve into a new observer with a new future in that domain. This is not static, though, as we are, after all, human liquid accordions, always expanding/contracting, always practicing something. As we navigate the world, we have the opportunity for this to happen all over again as our observer navigates the world.

New Shape
(New Observer)
SELPH
Length, Width, Depth, Commitment

A simple analogy will serve to make this more clear.

Imagine standing on the side of a body of water that looks very much like a swimming pool. The side you are standing on is known, and although it may be uncomfortable or ineffective, it is *known* and, on some level, familiar. This is the shape *you are now in,* and if you stay on this side of the pool you are practicing, and becoming more and more familiar and embodied with, this shape.

However, for whatever reason, you decide to jump into the water. This is the unbounded state where you are not on the old side of the pool, but you are not at the other side of the pool either. In fact, when you jump in, even if you want to go back to the old side of the pool, you can never completely get back there. As this is happening, the new side of the pool—because you are in the water—now cannot be seen, and the water you are now in seems to be deep and bottomless. Your body is uncomfortable, and like the feeling of not knowing how to swim, your body is flailing around to find some sort of dry land on the other side. The sooner the better, so when we get swimming, we head to the nearest visible piece of land (the other side of the proverbial pool).

If, by choice, you stay in the water and practice treading water for a bit (a somatic practice), it is possible that the other side of the pool will become more visible and the path to get there becomes clearer. This does not mean it will be easy, but it will become clearer as to how to get to the other side of the pool, where you wish to be. This is where

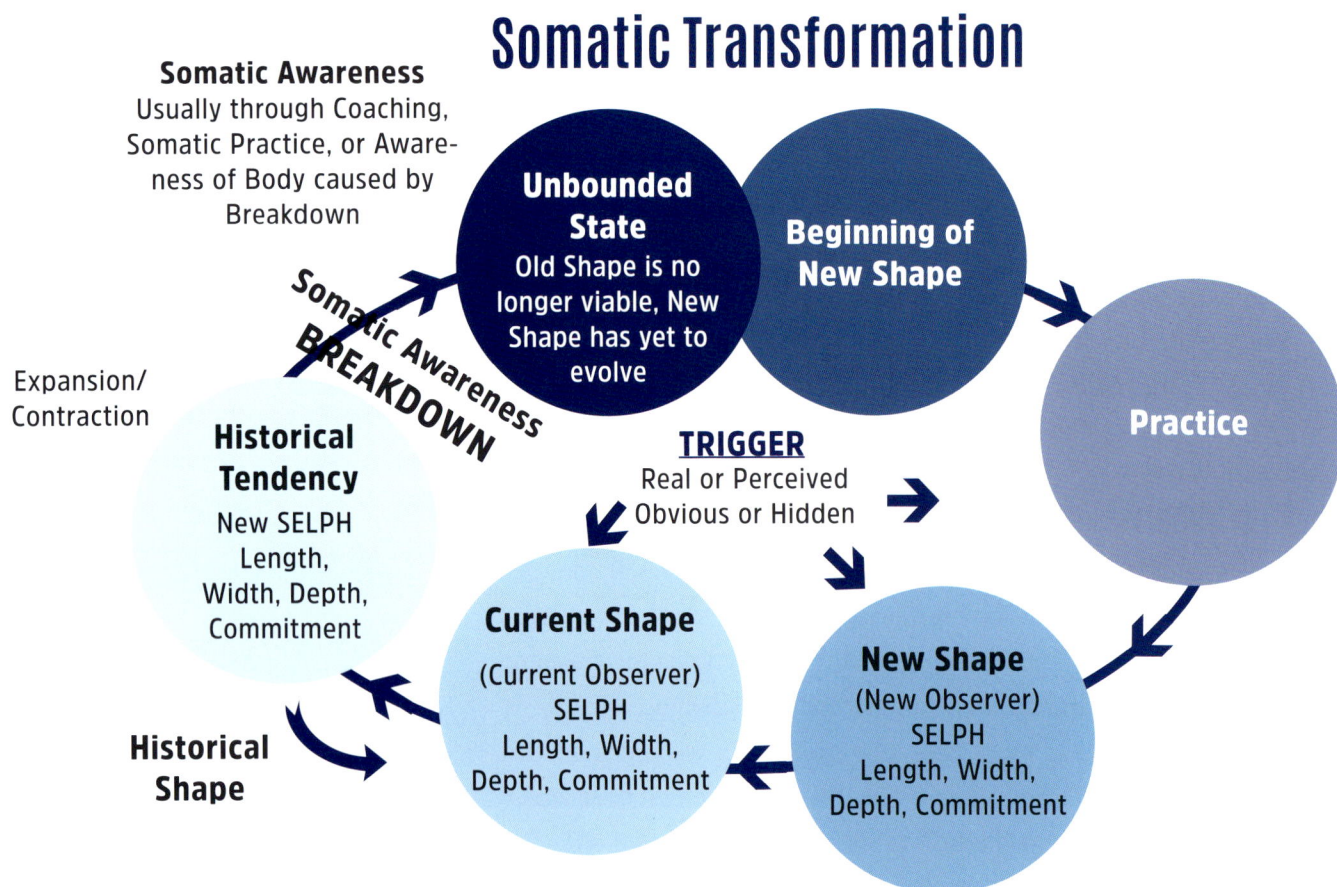

Somatic Transformation

Somatic Awareness
Usually through Coaching, Somatic Practice, or Awareness of Body caused by Breakdown

Somatic Awareness
BREAKDOWN

Expansion/
Contraction

Unbounded State
Old Shape is no longer viable, New Shape has yet to evolve

Beginning of New Shape

Practice

Historical Tendency
New SELPH
Length, Width, Depth, Commitment

TRIGGER
Real or Perceived
Obvious or Hidden

Current Shape
(Current Observer)
SELPH
Length, Width, Depth, Commitment

New Shape
(New Observer)
SELPH
Length, Width, Depth, Commitment

Historical Shape

the idea of practice for the sake of practicing serves to create a new, more effective, observer.

Once you are on the other side and the new shape has emerged, it is possible that in times of stress, chaos, or in the presence of the former trigger, that the old historical tendency will show up in your body and you will be back in the pool. With the new awareness, though, the water will not be as deep, and the ability to see and access the new side of the pool will be more embodied. Then you can leave the unbounded state of water you have assessed you are in.

The New Somatic Shape

At some point in the practice, we embody the new somatic shape, and it becomes our new normal and the shape we navigate the world in. That is, until we experience new triggers, and we get to practice all over again. Ahh, to be a liquid accordion . . .

New Shape
(New Observer)
SELPH
Length, Width,
Depth, Commitment

Breathing, the Fundamental Somatic Practice

"Feelings come and go like clouds in a windy sky. Conscious breathing is my anchor."
Thich Nhat Hang[38]

What is the one thing we have done every second we have been alive? What is the one thing we will do until that moment we die? The answer: *breathing*. That's right; we have been breathing all our lives and will continue to breathe until we die. Sounds simple enough, but ask performance specialists or elite athletes and you might understand that it is not just that we breathe, but rather *how* we breathe that determines how we show up in our bodies. Volumes have been written on the power of breathing and the biological aspects behind it. In our case, we will keep things simple.

As human beings we cannot control our heart rate, but we can control our breathing, which will then affect our heart rate. We therefore look at breathing as the fundamental centering technique; it is the one thing we can do to affect our shape, our physiology, and our well-being in the moment. Because of this, breathing is a wonderful foundational centering for both coach and coachee.

There are many different breathing techniques one can access. Many techniques in disciplines such as yoga, martial arts, and other meditative practices are available and beyond the scope of this book. For our sake we start with a simple breathing exercise. It is called the 6/6/3 technique. It works like this:

- Inhale deeply for 6 seconds.

- Exhale for 6 seconds.

- Do this three times.

This process takes a total of 36 seconds to complete, so for those of you who feel you do not have enough time for this in a typical day, can you find 1/2,400th of a day to try this? Of course you can. This is a simple practice for coaches to help coachees, during a call, to quickly center. A few fine points about the technique:

- When breathing in and out, be sure to allow the body to relax with the breathing.
- Imagine the air, on the inhale, reaching all parts of your body.
- On the exhale, imagine the air coming from all parts of your body.
- Be sure to breathe in and out through the nostrils—not the mouth.

When to Use the 6/6/3 Breathing Technique

The 6/6/3 breathing technique can be used at any time in the coaching conversation when a coachee is off-center. It is especially effective for the coachee to employ as a practice for themselves between coaching conversations.

A simple practice for the coachee can be to do this at least three times per day. Yes, centering can be as simple as breathing.

THIRTY

Centering Techniques

"At the center of your being you have the answer;
you know who you are and you know what you want."
Lao Tzu

As was discussed, there are many different centering techniques based on many different disciplines. If you have expertise in any of these practices, they can be utilized with the coachee as is or modified to meet the situation of the coach-coachee relationship. Whatever the technique, here are some simple guidelines for you the coach as you lead your coachee through a call.

Tailor the centering technique to the coachee and the current situation. When you are in a situation in a coaching call where you, the coach, assess that centering may help create awareness with the coachee, trust the wisdom of your body and tailor the centering to meet the situation. For instance, in a short coaching session of, say, 30 minutes, you might only have time for a 30-second centering, or because it is a longer session, you might do a deep centering practice for 5-10 minutes, and that becomes a huge takeaway for the coachee. Allow the coachee's new shape and awareness to inform you on how long to have the coachee practice centering.

Leverage the coachee's current observer and do not start a call with centering. Although some may disagree with this idea, a great move can be to not begin a call with centering. If the coachee shows up to the call rushed, triggered, or in their conditioned tendency, one school of thought is to have the coachee center to get them present for the call. A different way to look at it, however, is to leverage the coachee's off-centeredness to have them declare their breakdown for the call in their current off-centeredness. This is a possible way of observing for them, anyway, and later in the call it is the actual centering which can be the powerful new awareness that may help them become a new observer.

Lead the centering from center yourself. Regardless of the nature of the call, it is critical that you, the coach, lead the call from a more centered place so that you are not triggered or in a historical tendency as you coach. You can better help the coachee center if you yourself are already centered.

Use your body to assess the coachee's center. As discussed in a previous chapter, allow your body to be your somatic tuning fork to help you assess the coachee's center. If your body is not assessing the coachee's center, then listen to your body to help the coachee become aware of their observer.

The centering itself maybe the takeaway from the call. The simple act of centering can, of itself, be an extremely powerful takeaway and learning for many coachees. If someone lives in a body that does not experience center, just the simple awareness found in a 30-second centering practice can be powerful and create the opportunity for the coachee to have a new and powerful practice to take from the call.

When to Use the Centering Techniques

Centering techniques can be used in most coaching calls, and generally there are two situations where centering techniques can be extremely effective.

1) **The coachee is in a very uncentered state and living in a powerful mood/emotion, story, and body.** Centering can help the coachee become aware of their mood/emotion and story, and the body.

2) **The coachee is in a place where being centered will allow them to better be in choice about how they would like to show up in a situation.** For example, they need to be able to choose to be extremely resolute with a situation or, at the same time, they might need to be more open. By centering between each body shape, they can better choose a shape that will serve them.

The 4-Step Centering Technique

A simple foundational centering technique is called the 4-Step Centering Technique. As a practice this technique can take as short as about 30 seconds, and its length can be varied based on the situation and how long the coach assesses will serve the coachee. This technique can easily turn into a 5-to-10-minute technique. Do not focus so much on the time but more so on helping the coachee move through the four steps to find their center. The four steps:

1) **Breathe**. Start the 4-step centering technique by simply taking the coachee to their breathing. As with the 6/6/3 breathing technique, simply have the coachee begin by breathing three deep 6-second inhalations/6-second exhalations. Here is a sample script for the coach:

"Take three deep and powerful breaths. As you do, allow the breath to fill your body, breathing in for 6 seconds, and as you exhale, take the same 6 seconds to exhale and feel the breath leaving your body. Allow your focus to be on your breath."

2) **Be present in your body.** As the coachee is starting to breathe, have them be present in their body and really notice and connect with their body. Sample script:

"Allow yourself to just be in your body. Notice any awareness, sensations, temperatures, and/or tension or a lack of any of that. Allow your body to sink into and relate to the ground. Allow yourself to be open, present, and connected to those around you."

3) **Center yourself in four directions.** At this point we want to help the coachee find their length (vertical), width (side to side), and depth (front to back), along with what the coachee cares about or is committed to (care/commitment). Sample script:

"Center in your length (vertical). This is your connection to your dignity as a human, neither above nor below others but all having worth (dignity). Your width (side to side): this is your connection with others and humanity as a whole (connection with others). Your depth (front to back): this is your connection to time and being present (time). Finally, connect with what you care about. This can be your bigger purpose and meaning (care/commitment)."

4) **Choose your emotions.** Lastly, check in with the coachee's moods/emotions. Is the emotional space they are currently embodying serving them? Are there different emotions that would serve them? Is there different space for the coachee to be in emotional choice. Sample script:

"How would you like to show up in the immediate situation? Choose the mood/emotion in your words, and allow it to come alive in your body. Feel where the mood/emotion resides in your body, and increase your focus there. Allow the mood/emotion to expand in all directions. Bring the mood/emotion alive, and let it fill up your body and those around you in the room and the world."

As shared before, this technique can be built upon and expanded to meet the needs of the coachee in the situation. Allow the wisdom of your observer to serve you in this technique.

The Scanner Technique

"As my awareness increases, my control over my own being increases."
William Schutz [39]

The scanner technique is a highly effective way to bring the body into coaching situations. The technique is about bringing the coachee on a scan of their body to create awareness of their current or future observer, one they would like to create. It can be highly effective with coachees who tend to get into their "story," as it effectively moves the coachee from the story to their body.

When to Use

The scanner technique can be used in many coaching situations, and it is often utilized in the arc of coaching to help the coachee create awareness of either their current breakdown/observer, and/or it can be used to help the coachee bring alive a desired future observer better equipped to navigate a situation or the future.

Somatic Safety

Whenever using a technique like the scanner technique, be sure to have permission from the coachee to explore their observer in this manner. It is possible that taking a coachee into their body may make the coachee uncomfortable, possibly even traumatic, and thus it is critical to ensure that the coachee knows they can stop the exercise at any point in the process.

Also, it is critical to the success of this technique that the coachee be in a place in which they can have privacy to be in their body and move as necessary. A sample way to do that, if you are coaching remotely, might be something along the lines of: "Are you in a place where you have privacy, will not be interrupted, and feel comfortable standing up and possibly moving around?"

Foundational Keys

As stated above, it is best to have the coachee do this exercise standing up in a location where the coachee can move freely and will not be observed or interrupted by others.

The following script is a starting point only. As you practice this technique, it is likely that you will interject your words and patterns of speech. This is not only acceptable but highly encouraged. Make this your own, but it is recommended to practice it as close to the script as possible, at least initially, until you get a foundational comfort with the practice.

Script

Once the timing is right for the scanner technique, the following script can be used:

Coach: "Would it serve you if we did an exercise to maybe reveal to you the observer that you are around this situation?"

[Coachee responds positively]

"Great. For this exercise I would ask you to stand up, and what I would like you to do now is to really bring alive the situation where you are feeling _____ [fill in with what the observer has described to you, such as being overwhelmed or angry with their boss, etc.].

"As you are doing this I want you to really bring alive the situation you described, feel it, embody it, allow it to live in your body. Allow your body to take the shape it was (is), to move like it was (is), to be in your body as you were (are) in the situation. As you are doing this, feel the emotions you felt (feel) in the situation and really get in the story of what you were (are) telling yourself in the situation."

"I am going to be quiet for about 30 seconds as you do this."

[Observe the coachee as they do this, and make a mental note of any actions, movements, or shifts in their body as they do. You are observing for things such as dropping their shoulders, closing their eyes, moving around, or lowering their head. There is not a right or wrong with this. Just allow yourself, as a coach, to notice these things. You will possibly bring up your observations later in the scanner technique.]

"Now, stay in this body. Do not shift from where you are. Also, do not go to language as we do this, we will have time to debrief later in the exercise."

"Imagine there is a scanner, like from a sci-fi movie, and as I move it through your body, notice what you are aware of—things like temperature, pressure, awareness, sensation, or a lack of any of those things. As you notice and become aware of them, do not change them. Just be aware of them, and move on with the scanner."

[Note to coach: at this point, make sure to slow down your speech so the coachee has time to be with each body location, allowing him or her enough time for awareness to happen.]

"Imagine the scanner starting at the top of your head. Notice: is your head up? Is it down?"

"Notice your forehead, your cheeks, your jaw. Is there tension there?"

"Notice your eyes. Are they open? Are they closed? If they are open, are they focused, or are they relaxed?"

"Now notice into your neck area. Is there tension?"

"Notice your shoulders. Are they up, are they down, are they forward, are they back?"

"Move to your back. Are you aware of anything there? Whatever you notice is fine; no need to change anything."

"Move now to you front, to your lungs. How is your breathing? Is it slow? Is it fast? Is it deep? Is it shallow? Just notice. There is not a right or a wrong."

"Now notice your heart area. Can you feel your heart beating? If so, is it slow? Is it fast?"

"Notice your internal organs. Do you feel anything? Is there a pit in your stomach? Are there butterflies in your stomach?"

"Feel into your arms. Are you aware of your arms? Are they crossed? Notice your hands. Are they relaxed? Are they clinched? Are they open?"

"Move to your pelvic region. Do you have awareness there? Are your hips forward? Are they back?"

"Down now into your legs. Do you feel your legs? How about your upper legs? Do they feel strong? Do they feel weak?"

"How about your knees? Your calves? Move to your feet. Are they planted firmly on the ground, or are you on your toes? Your heels? To one side or the other? Is your weight on one foot or both feet? No right or wrong; just notice."

"Finally, feel the energy in your body if you can. Can you feel it? Is it moving slow? Is it fast? Is it located in one area of your body? Is it blocked anywhere? Does it feel contained within you? Or does it feel more external?"

"Take a minute and really shake out our body and come back, and let's have a conversation about what you experienced."

[Allow the coachee to really let go of the observer they just were and, if necessary, have them do some sort of quick centering exercise.]

Debrief of the Scan

After the coachee sits down, begin the debrief. The following script is a starting point for debriefing, and the curiosity, skill, and abilities of the coach will obviously guide the conversation in a direction that will serve the coachee.

"Before we debrief, I just want to make sure that nothing came from the scan of your body that you assess we need to address before we go any further?"

[Assuming not, continue with the script.]

"So, what showed up in your body when we did the scan? And, as you do this, I ask that initially you only share the sensations, awareness, pressure, temperature, or energy that showed up. Do not get into any stories or assessments of what that actually means."

[Allow the coachee to share.

As the coachee shares their experiences, you may add in any questions, assessments, or perceptions that you as the coach noticed when you were observing the coachee in the process.

For instance, let's say the coachee shares: "I felt really tired and heavy."

The coach can respond with something like: "Is there anywhere specifically in your body that you feel the heaviness?" Or, "Tired sounds like an assessment. What specifically do you feel that causes you to make that assessment?"

Also, you can explore any assessments you as the coach have about what you noticed that the coachee did not address, such as:

"I noticed you spent the majority of the time with your head looking down and your eyes focused on your feet. Any awareness of that?"

The goal of this part of the debrief is to help the coachee gain somatic insights and awareness. There is not a right or wrong way to do this, but here a few key points about this part.

- Many times the coachee will try to take the conversation into their story or assessments of what they were feeling. The key is to simply have them focus on what sensations, awareness, etc. they were experiencing—not their interpretation of what it means. This will be addressed soon enough.

- Try not to get into coaching or a deep conversation about somatic awareness. It can be tempting to jump into action and try to get the conversations around new actions or exploring here. Trust the process of the scanner technique.

Once the conversation has come to a bit of a conclusion of what the coachee experienced in the scanning, move the dialogue along in the following manner.]

"Now, you have shared some of the sensations you experienced in the scan. If you were to assign moods, emotions, or moods and emotions that you assess describe what you were experiencing, what moods, emotions, or moods and emotions, would you share?"

[Allow time for the coachee to put the sensations into words and to share the emotions they are experiencing, making sure, as much as possible, to not put any words in the coachee's mouth.

At this point it is okay to explore a bit, though, about the moods/emotions the coachee referenced, but do not spend too much time here. Also, do not allow the coachee to get into their story.]

"So, of the [number of, provide here] emotions you mentioned [relist each emotion], which of those would you say best describes the emotion that dominated the experience?"

[Allow the coachee to respond.]

"So you feel that the best descriptor would be [mood or emotion]? Is that correct?"

[Coachee responds affirmatively.]

"Can we call this your [mood/emotion / coachee name]?"

Example:

"So, of the three emotions you mentioned—anger, frustration, and a bit of guilt—which of those would you say best describes the emotion that dominated the experience?"

Coachee: "I would say anger!"

Coach: "So you feel that the best descriptor would be anger? Is that correct?"

Coachee responds affirmatively.

"Can we call this Angry Mary?"

Allow the coachee to respond.

"Great. And when [stated emotion/coachee name; such as "Angry Mary"] shows up, in one or two sentences, and one or two sentences only, what is the story, the theme, or the meta-story that is running through your mind in this situation?"

[Coachee responds: make sure you challenge the coachee to not get into the story but rather to keep it to one or two sentences only.]

"So a big question: what is possible when [stated emotion/coachee name; such as "Angry Mary"] shows up in this situation, or situations, like this?"

[Allow the coachee to share. Many times, when this is first done, the coachee sees the limitations of their observer in the previous situation. Have a conversation with the coachee to explore the limitations of the old observer, and have them share any insights they are now aware of if this will serve them.

With the old observer revealed, the coaching conversation is at a crossroads. One direction the coach can offer the coachee is to see if the coachee would like to explore some aspect of the old observer; or, check in with the coachee to see if they assess that the old observer would not serve them, and see if they would like to explore a different, more effective, more powerful observer. The conversation can go something like this:]

"My assessment is there might be a couple directions we can explore with this if you are open to hearing where I assess you might take it?"

[Coachee responds in the affirmative.]

"We could, if you assess it would serve you, explore the old or current observer you are/were of [stated emotion/coachee name i.e. "Angry Mary"]. Or, if you would rather, we can explore what the world would look like if you showed up as 'your best self,' or in a manner which would allow you to best deal with the breakdown situation. Which do you assess would better serve you?"

[It is likely that most times the coachee will choose to explore ways to show up as their best self to navigate the situation. Should the coachee want to explore their current observer, allow the conversation to go in that direction. If that is the case, the conversation may leave the scanner technique and evolve into more traditional, linguistic-based coaching.

Assuming the coachee chooses to continue down the path of the scanner technique, continue the conversation. Sample script:]

"So what I propose is that we do the scanner technique again, but this time I want to offer for you to bring [coachee name] at your best. There are a few ways we can do this. One is to explore a time in your past when you were at your best, a time when you felt like you could take on the world, a time when things just flowed and seemed to be effortlessly falling into place. Another route we can take is for you to find the 'you' that is as far away from [old mood/emotion coachee name] as you can get, or even choose how you would like to show up in this situation. There is not a right or a wrong, though. Choose an observer that you assess would really serve you in this situation. Can you think of how you would like to show up?"

[Allow time for the coachee to think this through, and a conversation may even need to emerge to explore this. When the coachee feels they are ready, start with the following script. You will notice it is fundamentally the same as the first script, but with slight differences.]

Example:

"As before, as you do this, I will be quiet for about 30 seconds to allow you to really bring alive the new observer of you, as the best 'you,' for the situation."

[Allow 30 seconds to pass. As you are doing this, observe the coachee to see what you, as the coach, notice is different in their body from the first scan, and make note of it for the following debrief.]

"Imagine again the scanner, and as I walk it through your body, notice any sensations, temperatures, awareness, pressures, or a lack of any of those things. As you do it this time, you may use your old body as a reference point, or you may choose to not do so. Again, as you notice these things, do not shift your body, just be in this body and make a mental note of it. Also, I ask you not to go to language."

[Important note to coach: again, at this point, slow down your voice to allow the coachee to have time to be in this new body.] As coach, continue:

"Imagine the scanner again at the top of your head. Is your head up, or is it down?"

"What do you notice, if anything, in your forehead, your cheeks, your jaw?"

"Are your eyes open or closed this time? If they are open, are they focused? Are they relaxed? Are they scanning?"

"Now move into your neck area. Is there tension there?"

"Down into your shoulders. Are they the same as before? Are they up, are they down, are they back, are they forward?"

"Move to your back. Do you notice anything? Again, no right or wrong, just notice."

"Move your awareness to the front of your body, in your chest. What do you notice about your breathing? Is it slow? Is it fast? Is it deep? Is it shallow? Allow yourself to be in your breathing."

"What about your heart? Can you feel it? If so, what do you notice?"

"Move to your midsection, your internal organs. Is there any pit in your stomach, or is there any awareness at all?"

"Notice your pelvic region. Is there any awareness there?"

"Move down into your legs; do you notice your legs? Start with your quads, then your knees, and into your calves. What do you notice, if anything?"

"How about your feet? What do you notice in your feet? Is your weight distributed evenly? Is it to one side? Is one foot more forward versus the other? Just notice. There is not a right or a wrong."

"Finally, what do you notice about your energy now? Is it flowing differently than before? Is it slow, or slower? Is it fast, or faster? Is it more external, out-flowing? Or more internal, more inflowing?"

"Do not shake your body out this time. Stay in this body, then come back. And then we can debrief."

Debrief of the Scan

After the coachee sits down, begin the debrief. The following script is a starting point for debriefing, and again, the curiosity, skill, and abilities of the coach will obviously guide the conversation in a direction that will serve the coachee.

"What did you notice this time? Was there anything different?"

[At this point, it is likely the coachee will have some sort of new awareness. Allow him or her to share as much as they want, but it is critical to keep them focused on what was the new awareness in their body—such as new sensations, any change in temperature or pressure—and not on their interpretation or story of what it means. As the coachee shares, allow space for questions to dig deeper and to explore any new awarenesses.

As before, if the coachee shares assessments of meaning or assigns emotions to the feelings, steer the coachee back to the actual sensations or awarenesses.]

Coaching Tip

As you are in the conversation of the debrief, make a mental note of any of the following. Note any profound awarenesses of sensations that showed up in either of the scans in the following areas:

- the head
- the eyes
- the jaw
- the shoulders
- breathing
- the hands
- the feet

Note any extreme differences in a specific body part between the two scans, such as:

- eyes that were focused in the first scan and very relaxed in the second scan
- jaw that was clenched in the first scan and relaxed in the second
- arms that were crossed in the first scan and relaxed in second
- other body part differences that were extreme

The purpose of making these notes is these awarenesses/differences are the places where the coachee can practice. (See the rest of the text for more details.)

"So, you shared that you were aware of [name the body awareness]. Are there any other sensations, temperature changes, pressures, awarenesses, or energies that you wish to share?"

[Allow the coachee to respond. When complete, continue the conversation.]

"As we did before, if you were to assign moods, emotions, or moods and emotions to what you just experienced, what would you say you experienced?"

[Allow space for the coachee to share and, if necessary, dig a bit deeper with coaching questions. However, do not, if possible, put words in the coachee's mouth. If necessary or applicable, as a coaching move, you can share this.]

"As you were doing the second scan, the mood that showed up for me was [insert the mood you observed]. Is there any resonating with that for you?"

[Many times, this will either help the coachee name the moods/emotions or help them further clarify what the mood/emotion is.]

"You mentioned [number] moods/emotions [now state each emotion]. Which of those would you say best describes the emotion that dominated the experience?"

[Let the coachee respond.]

"Is that the best descriptor [mood or emotion]?"

[The coachee will likely respond affirmatively.]

"So, can we call this your [mood/emotion / coachee name]?" After an affirmative from the coachee . . .

"Awesome. When [stated emotion / coachee name] shows up, in one or two sentences, and one or two sentences only, what is the story, the theme, or the meta-story that is running through your mind in this situation?"

[The coachee responds. Again, make sure you challenge the coachee to not get into a lengthy story, but rather that they keep it to one or two sentences only.]

"So, a big question: what would be possible when [stated emotion / coachee name] shows up in the old situation?"

[Allow the coachee to share. As they share the second observer, it is likely they will have a much more powerful and situationally effective way of viewing the world. The goal now is to keep the coachee in this current "best self" observer to help them transition to practices to serve them. Many times when the new observer shows up, the old situation or breakdown does not seem as daunting, overwhelming, or restricting—and the coachee is already in take-action mode.]

The *Liquid Accordion* in Action « « « « « « « «

It could pay to be lazy . . .

For those of you who like to frown, the good news is that you are getting a facial workout. It takes 43 muscles in the face working together to frown. On the other hand, it pays to be lazy—it only takes 17 muscles working together to smile.

Practices

Let's go on with some sample scripts that will deal with practices.

"So, what are some practices you could start to do that would allow [best-self / name] to show up to deal with the situation?"

[The goal at this point is to help the coachee see the power of somatic practices. It is common for the coachee to say something like:]

- "I think I need to practice putting notes by my computer so I will see X."

- "I need to have conversations with my team about Y."

- "I must be more proactive around Z."

The challenge with practices like this is that, though they are well-intentioned, the coachee would likely be practicing them from the old/current observer, not the new, more powerful observer. To shift this and help the coachee really create a new, more powerful self, the practices are to be done in, with, and through the body. The practices now should be tied to the new observer body shape. For instance, if the coachee realizes that in their new "best-self" observer . . .

- . . . their head was up, and their eyes scanning more, and . . .
- . . . their shoulders were up, chest expansive, and . . .
- . . . their jaw was relaxed . . .

Then, they now want to make their practices . . .

- lifting their head and scanning more with their eyes;
- tilting their shoulders up and back; also, leaving their chest more expansive;
- relaxing their jaw.

The new somatic practices will bring them to their new "best-self" observer and will allow space for that observer to take the new actions needed. A useable method can be to have the coachee explore the old situation with the new somatic practices and, in the next coaching conversation, explore what was revealed with the new somatic observer.

One last thought about practices in the scanner technique, or any somatic practice: when exploring the body as a domain of practice, there are what we call the Big Seven areas to practice in.

The Big Seven

When we are creating somatic practices from the scanner technique, or any technique for that matter, the following seven places are great areas of focus:

- Head: tilt it up or down
- Eyes: open or close more, focus or relax
- Jaw: relax or put tension in
- Breathing: slow/fast, deep/shallow
- Shoulders/chest: rotate shoulders back/open and expand chest area
- Hands: open/closed, relaxed/tension, palms open/closed
- Feet: on toes, heels, or entire foot

Like any coaching techniques, the scanner technique takes practice to master and become proficient in.

A quick check-in: do a short scanner on yourself to see where you are in your body as you do this technique.

Observing the Liquid Accordion in the Wild: Tension-Filled Interactions

The next time you're in a situation that involves others where there seems to be noticeable tension and conflict, try to relax your jaw and be in the conversation. Really allow your lower jaw to hang and not have any tension.

What does this do to the conversation and the tension of others? Is there a real desire to clench your jaw? What does this tell you about the jaw and conflict? Do you think a boxer in a boxing match would have their jaw relaxed or tense? What about in tender moments? Is your jaw likely relaxed, or is there tension in the jaw and the jaw shut?

Coaching the Liquid Accordion

Coachee #1: Norman—The Scanner Technique to Raise Awareness

If you remember back in chapter 1, we were introduced to Norman, the 45-year-old engineer who lived in his head. When he came to his coach to learn how to access his body to become a new observer, the coach saw an opportunity to use the scanner technique to help him create awareness. The conversation led Norman to declare a breakdown around his relationship with his boss concerning an unfinished project. The coach walked Norman through his body, through the scanner technique, for the first time.

The practice allowed Norman a place to realize that he did not have much somatic awareness. He did, however, become aware that when he explored the breakdown situation he was observing at work, he had tension in his lower back, shoulders, neck, and forehead. When the coach led him to explore his emotional state, he shared that he was in a state he would call "Resentment Norman," and his story was that his boss "had screwed me over."

This awareness led the coach to offer Norman to do the scanner technique again. This time, when Norman chose an observer that would serve him, he decided on "Ambition Norman." In "Ambition Norman" he felt like he could better have the conversation needed with his boss to declare a breakdown. In the scanner technique the second time, Norman had much more awareness of his body. He was aware that in Ambition Norman his shoulders were back and his chest wide open and expansive. He was aware that his head was up and his range of vision much more expansive, he had a playfulness in his legs, and there was an energy pushing him forward into action. The new Ambition

Norman awareness allowed Norman to create new practices involving his body such as centering, opening his chest, and grounding his feet prior to the conversation with his boss. This new observer allowed Norman and his boss to have a conversation, which had been missing, and in fact had been needed for some time.

After much practice, Norman can now access ambition and the corresponding emotional state with little work. He has even stated that he is more ambitious overall.

THIRTY-TWO

Somatic Role Playing (SRP)

*"Sometimes you have to play the role of a fool to fool
the fool who thinks they're fooling you."*
Anonymous

Somatic Role Playing (SRP) is a great way to bring the body into play in coaching conversations. The basic idea is that the coach and coachee embody the coachee and another person in relationship with the coachee. The purpose of SRP is to have the coachee experience either how their body shows up in a situation with another, or for the coachee to experience how another person may experience their interactions with the coachee. This technique has room for variations which may apply to each situation, but the foundational ideals are the same.

When to Use

This technique can be used when the coachee is in a situation where they are struggling with another person in a relationship—i.e., work, boss/peer, or personal lives such as with a family member or significant other. In this exercise they can either explore their current observer, the other person's current observer, or their future, desired observer. For the coach to successfully be a partner in SRP, it is important that the coach himself or herself somewhat embody different shapes or styles so they can play the character of one of the role players.

Setting the Stage

As a coaching conversation unfolds, it is possible that the coach will observe the coachee in some sort of somatic shape or combination of a shape we have previously discussed. This shape will arise in the context of a current relationship such as with a boss or significant other. As the coach becomes aware of a shape for the coachee through the coaching dialogue, an opportunity to explore shape, with the coachee, will likely arise. The coach can offer SRP to help the coachee create awareness of his or her current observer. Some of the possibilities include:

Coachee Role Plays:	**Coach Role Plays:**
Themselves: current observer	Other Person: current observer
Themselves: future observer	Other Person: potential future observer
Other Person: current observer	Coachee: current observer
Other Person: future observer*	Coachee: future observer

* Based on how the coachee would show up as a future observer

The coaching will sometimes involve a few rounds of SRP depending on the situation. A likely scenario will be helping the coachee see his or her current observer, and then a second scenario will involve the coachee experiencing a different future observer. In the role-play the coach and coachee will develop a scenario that is relevant to the coachee and the other person—for instance, they may role-play a feedback session. Depending on the time available, each scenario can be 3 to 7 minutes to allow space for the coachee to experience his or her somatic shape and awareness in the situation.

Example: Mary is coaching Tom. Tom has an Amiable Body Shape and tends to avoid conflict, especially with his boss, Amy. Amy has an extreme Results Body Shape and tends to be direct and to the point. She tends to get easily triggered by Tom when Tom shows up as amiable and will not take a stand on issues. Tom needs to have a conversation with Amy about a breakdown his team is having about a new product.

Round 1

Coachee (Tom) role-plays: Themselves: current observer; Tom as he shows up in an Amiable Body

Coach (Mary) role-plays: Other Person (Amy): current observer; Results Shape: Amy is triggered

Round 2

Coachee (Tom) role-plays: Themselves: future observer; Tom shows up in a Resolute Body

Coach (Mary) role-plays: Other Person (Amy): future observer; Results Shape: Amy responds as how she might if Tom shows up in a more Results Shape

Round 3

Coachee (Tom) role-plays: Themselves: future observer; Tom as he shows up in a more Centered Shape

Coach (Mary) role-plays: Other Person (Amy): future observer; Results Shape: Amy responding how she might show up if Tom shows up in a more Centered Shape

It is likely in Round 2 Tom will need practice in the Results Body Shape as he will likely be very much a beginner and need the practice. It is okay and helpful if the coach shares some distinctions and practices for Tom to be in a more Results Shape. This might include clenching his jaw, leaning his body forward, focusing his eyes, and practicing the more results-shaped body.

After the coachee has experienced the new body shape, in the second round it is possible to try the scenario again from either the new practiced shape or with an entirely different shape.

Allow your creativity as a coach to come into play in the SRP. Trust your body and how it shows up for you as you help your coachee role-play.

Coaching the Four Body (Plus One) Shapes

"Working myself into a position of total versatility, so that I can do anything I want to do at the time I want to do it. Whether I do it or not is another question."

Elliott Erwitt[40]

The four basic body shapes can be an effective way to help a coach see how their current shape/observer is determining how they see the world as an observer. The basic idea in this coaching practice is to have the coachee shift from their current shape/observer to one or more shapes/observers and have them see what new possibilities arise as they become the new shape/observer.

When to Use the Four Bodies Technique

The four bodies technique can be used any time the coachee is in a current shape/observer limiting them from seeing other possibilities. A near-requirement is that the coachee be in a place where they have privacy and a bit of space to move around in their bodies.

How to Use the Four Bodies Technique

As the coaching unfolds and it becomes apparent to the coach that the coachee has a body shape that is not serving them, or at the least is limiting their ability to be a new observer or take actions, the coach can offer this technique as a potential path to new learning.

Assuming that the coachee is open to the practice, set it up in a manner somewhat aligned with what follows.

- Have the coachee scan their body using the body scanning technique or some variation. The goal is to help the coachee become aware of their current observer, specifically how they are showing up somatically and in their body.

- Through dialogue with the coachee, assess or offer if there is one or more body shapes that would serve them. It is possible that the coachee will not see options; therefore, the coach can suggest one or more (but not too many) different observers or shapes.

- The coach would then have the coachee stand up, if possible, and break their space into a number of sections corresponding to the total of body shapes to be practiced (including the current shape). For example, if the coachee is in a results body shape, and they and the coach determine an open or a stable body would serve them, divide the room into three sections. It is important that the coachee can physically move to the new section for the learning. If it is not possible to move around, have them do this exercise in the same place.

- Have the coachee embody their current shape and share with the coach.
    1) their somatic awareness
    2) their assessments of what moods/emotions they are in
    3) their assessment of their story

- Have the coachee jump or move to one of the other sections and embody the new shape/observer. It may be necessary for the coach to share with the coachee some suggestions of how to embody the other shape, such as relaxing their body, focusing their eyes, etc. The goal is for the coachee to truly embody the new shape/observer. As the coachee is in the new body, have them share with the coach:
    1) their somatic awareness
    2) their assessments of what moods/emotions they are in
    3) their assessment of their story

- Repeat for a different shape/observer if necessary.

- Do this as many times as necessary to help the coachee see:
    1) what the coachee can do to shift their observer, mostly in their body
    2) what are they seeing differently as a result of the new shape

- This process itself might be the takeaway for the coachee. Not that there is a specific body shape/observer that is best, but rather to help them see that they have choices as to how to show up as a shape/observer in a situation.

- Another variation of this is to have the coachee make a declaration of something as simple as "no" or "I will" in the different body shapes/observers to help them become aware of their current and potential future observers.

Coaching the Liquid Accordion

Coachee #2: Rebecca—Coaching to the Four Bodies to Raise Awareness

Since Rebecca had a deep awareness of her body, her coach knew that helping her access her body would be a practice she would likely relish and take to. In her coaching conversation Rebecca became aware that she spent much of her time in an amiable body shape. Her body was open and inviting to others. She would spend time in interactions with others smiling to the extent that others would say she was, at times, *too* nice and *too* giving.

As Rebecca was aware with her body, she quickly connected that her amiable body, while serving her in relating with others, was limiting her advancement at work. She also realized that the results body shape would really serve her at times in meetings. To do this she created a simple practice of using the pivot points of the jaw (see chapter 37) by clenching her jaw and, while sitting in a meeting, putting tension in her hands and feet to better stand her ground with others. Through this awareness, Rebecca had a quite profound discovery to see that, just by adding a few simple somatic practices, she could create new results with others.

Breathe to Blend (BTB)

"When you change the way you look at things, the things you look at change."
Max Planck[41]

Breathe to Blend (BTB) is a technique to help a coachee deal with being in a triggered somatic shape. It is a practice that can be used in the coaching conversation and then be a powerful practice for the coachee to practice in real time in situations where they have been triggered and are now in an historical tendency. The practice has six steps, which are done in order, to help the coachee go from a triggered, historical shape to a shape which will serve them going forward in situations that have triggered them, or in other like situations. The six steps:

1. Breathe

2. Center

3. Acknowledge

4. Choose

5. Embody

6. Blend

Each Step in Detail

1. **Breathe:** The first step in the BTB, like the title states, is to breathe. Obviously, the coachee is already breathing, but the practice is to take *three* deep nose breaths alternating between *six* seconds of breathing, followed by six seconds breathing out. Doing this three times will, in theory, take 36 seconds to complete. When one becomes more adept at BTB, this can be shortened as the practitioner gets better at regulating their body through breathing.

2. **Center:** This part of the practice, as the participant gets more experience or has their own centering techniques, can be varied using different centering techniques. Fundamentally, though, the practice is for the coachee to center to a place where they are actually in choice and can observe the situation in a manner which is not driven by their current shape or emotional disposition.

3. **Acknowledge:** The coachee is acknowledging to themselves that 1) they are in an emotionally triggered shape; and 2) this emotionally triggered state does not serve them. This opens up step 4.

4. **Choose:** The coachee is in a centered state to choose how they would like to show up to the situation in three domains: *body, emotions,* and *language* (BEL). The coachee does not need to have clarity in each of the domains; they can have even just a vague clarity of one of the domains. It is in the next step that clarity comes alive.

5. **Embody:** The coachee begins to shift into the somatic shape they would like to address the breakdown in, or the emotional state they would like to be in. Whatever path is chosen, the practice for the coachee is to literally shift their body to the actual shape. This can be a body that is more open, more grounded, more ambitious, more resolute, more loving, etc. The key is that, in the moment, the coachee starts to embody and feel the new shape/emotional state. Once the coachee is in the new body shape or emotional state, the coachee is ready for the last step.

6. **Blend:** The coachee enters into conversation or interaction with their person or trigger, all the while keeping their new chosen shape and, at the same time, blending with the other person or trigger. The practice for the coachee is to be in their new shape and, as the other shape/emotions are confronted, still maintain their new shape. This can take practice as, in the moment, the coachee's old historical-conditioned shape, a shape the coachee likely knows well and has practiced many times, will likely show up. Let's look at an example.

Example: Steve

Steve is a likable, kind, and loving leader who wants to do all he can to lead his team. His body shape is expressive, and he tends to get fired up and triggered from conflict, especially when it comes to his boss, Dan. As Steve puts it, "Dan gets my goat!" Steve is especially good at playing the victim and goes into full attack mode when he is triggered. Dan has a very results-shaped body and, if asked, would say that he does not get into the pettiness of conflict, that he simply jumps in and wants to get to the point and solve the problem without emotions getting in the way.

Lately there has been tension in the relationship. If you ask Steve, he would say it is because Dan is being a jerk concerning the new project they are working on, and when Dan "micromanages" him, Steve believes, there is much tension in the relationship.

In their coaching session, Steve and his coach explored through the Breathe to Blend Exercise how to navigate Steve's relationship. The coaching started when Steve's coach, Molly, role-played Dan in their interactions. To get Steve into it she had Steve stand and face away from her. Molly stood behind Steve at about 45 degrees to him, just out of his periphery vision. She then grabbed his right forearm with a bit of force (with Steve's permission) and at the same time, said aloud "Steve, your project is late again!" (Something Steve said Dan might say to him which would trigger him.) Steve's body immediately triggered and resentment showed up. Steve, through the practice, first:

- Took 3 deep **Breaths**

- **Centered** in length, width, and depth

- **Acknowledged** to himself that he was triggered

- **Choose** to **Embody** emotions of openness and playfulness

- Turned to Molly (role-playing Dan) and **Blended** with Molly to start the conversation with "Dan" by making a request for different conversation

A bit awkward and slow to practice it at first, Steve shared with Molly after a few practices that he could now see a potential conversation with Dan.

At the next coaching conversation, Steve excitedly shared with Molly that, although he still sometimes get triggered by Dan, he now uses the BTB move in the situations and that he and Dan have had several much more open and effective conversations on how to work together. Steve shared that Dan even mentioned that there was something new in their conversations and that Dan felt like they were working better together.

When to Use the BTB

The BTB can be effectively used in situations when the coachee is in a recurring situation with other people or relationships that create a triggered-historical tendency/shape in the coachee within that relationship. Because of this historical shape, the coachee finds they are an observer with a historical shape that does not serve them in this relationship.

THIRTY-FIVE

Expand/Contract

"Time expands, then contracts, all in tune with the stirrings of the heart."
Haruki Murakami[42]

The Expand/Contract Coaching Technique is used to help the coachee create awareness in his or her body. It is, at its most simple, a practice of either expanding (relaxing) or contracting (clenching) certain muscles to bring awareness to that specific body area. It is tied to both Shakras and body armoring and is designed by the coach to help the coachee bring the wisdom of that part of the body into play for the coachee.

When to Use the Expand/Contract Technique

Again, the expand/contract technique can be used to help the coachee create awareness in his or her body. Because of this, it is a technique that is used more often with coachees who have limited somatic awareness. The practice takes them into their body and has them expand and/or contract specific muscles to bring awareness to the muscles and that specific part of the body.

How to Use the Expand/Contract Technique

For the expand/contract technique to be used by the coach, the coach needs to have some awareness of the coachee's body. The idea is that the coachee is aware they are unaware of their body, and they have a general knowledge that this technique could help them shift their shape/observer. This creates a situation where the coach can, through dialogue, help the coachee start to connect with and become aware of their body. For instance, a coachee may be unaware of the armoring in their face, specifically in their oral band. They are unaware of how their jaw is set and how it creates the armoring in this area. The coach can use the expand/contract technique in several ways. For instance:

- Have the coachee clench their jaw as tight as they can for ten seconds, then release the jaw and let it hang without tension. The coachee can then relax their facial muscles to see how the world looks with a relaxed jaw.

- Conversely, the coach may have the coachee clench their jaw and focus their eyes as they look at a problem. This will help the coachee focus on a point in front of himself or herself to create awareness about how to be more focused.

- The coach can have the coachee relax (expand) the muscles around their heart and, at the same time, the coachee can lightly connect their hand(s) to their heart to feel emotions in the region.

The main point of the expand/contract exercises is to help the coachee create awareness in their body in locations of which they may be unaware. The imagination and somatic intuition of the coach can create many different twists on the technique. As the coach practices these exercises with coachee, the coach will develop his or her own techniques in this practice.

THIRTY-SIX

Coaching to the Speech Acts

"The limits of my language means the limits of my world."
Ludwig Wittgenstein[43]

Coaching in, with, and through the body with speech acts is a way to bring awareness to the coachee about the congruency/lack of congruency of their BEL and what shifts are necessary and/or possible. We will explore each of the speech acts along with potential coaching moves of each. The basic premise is that when there is awareness in the coaching conversation, the coachee is at a place where there is a need for a specific speech act (a declaration, a request, sharing an assessment, etc.). However, be aware of this: the choice of the body shape to be in is just as critical as actually making a speech act. As an example, imagine a boss making a request to others to come to his office because he has an open door and "wants feedback," but the boss makes the request in a results body shape and in a clear mood of resentment. As you would imagine, it is not likely the boss's employees will see the request as a genuine one or be likely to come to the boss to share feedback. As the coachee explores speech acts in different body shapes, a few points will help.

- There is not one shape that is best for any of the speech acts. One does not always have to make a request from an open body shape or make a declaration from only the results body shape.

- Allow space for the coachee to "try on" the speech acts in different bodies. Create space for them to make a request, for instance, in different body shapes such as amiable and methodical bodies.

- It is likely the coachee will need to practice the speech act and preferred body shape many times before they become competent at it. They likely have been practicing the old body shape for years and are good at it. It likely will take time and practice to get to where they can actually do the speech act with a level of competence.

- Share with the coachee your assessments of what shows up for you as they practice the speech acts. Your assessments can help the coachee tweak what they actually practice and what shows up for you as a listener.

When to Use the Speech Acts Techniques

Speech acts techniques can be used in many situations with coachees and their specific speech acts.

Each of the speech acts are listed below with a definition of each. Examples of how to coach to that speech act, with potential body shapes, are also listed.

Declarations and the Body

Declaration: Something which is spoken by someone with the authority to make the statement, which opens up a new future or reality.

When this might be used: Declarations can be used by the coachee when they need to open up a new future.

Examples:

- An employee might declare that he or she is quitting their job.

- A person might declare that today is the day they begin a new workout routine.

- A person declares a relationship over.

The coachee can practice their declaration in a results body shape or a methodical body shape, along with either an amiable or spontaneous body shape to compare/contrast the declaration in a different shape.

Offers and the Body

Offer: When we put ourselves forward to take actions for others.

When this might be used: Offers might serve the coachee to take action to create a new shared future with another person.

Examples:

- An employee might offer to his boss to take on cleaning up part of the business that has been neglected.

- A person might offer to drive a friend to a job interview.

- A person might offer to cook dinner for a potential romantic interest.

The coachee then can practice their offers in an amiable body shape or a methodical body shape, compared to their current body shape.

Requests and the Body

Request: When we attempt to have someone do something for us.

When this might be used: Requests can be used by the coachee when they need help from others to create a shared future.

Examples:

- An employee might request that his boss give him feedback on how he is doing on a certain project.

- A person might request that a peer have a conversation about a business partnership.

- A person requests that a romantic partner starts inviting them to a group they have been previously excluded from.

The coachee can then practice their request in a results body shape or a spontaneous body shape. They then could practice an amiable or methodical shape to provide context.

Promises and the Body

Promise: When we commit our being to a shared future with others.

When this might be used: Promises can be used by the coachee when they commit to a future.

Examples:

- An employee might promise to her boss that she will be on time for future meetings.

- A person might promise to a friend that they will include them in future social gatherings.

- A person promises a romantic partner to listen more openly in the future.

The coachee can then practice their request in a results body shape or an open body shape, comparing that with a very closed body.

Assessments and the Body

Assessments: These are our opinions and judgments.

When this might be used: Assessments allow us to decide which actions will suit a situation.

Examples:

- An employee might make an assessment that the best future for him is to leave an organization for a new job offer.

- A person might assess that a friendship is becoming a romantic relationship, and then assess that it is not appropriate.

- A person assesses their romantic partner is not feeling appreciated, and the person can decide to take action accordingly.

The coachee can practice sharing their assessments in a results body shape or a centered body shape. They can then determine which shape will best serve them.

Assertions and the Body

Assertions: What is factual in our world with a universal standard.

When this might be used: Many times the breakdowns around assertions are that the person does not accept the fact of the assertion. It is the lack of acceptance that creates the actual breakdown.

Examples:

- An employee struggles to accept that she did not get a promotion. The assertion is that another person got the promotion. The practice is to accept that reality.

- A person struggles with the assertion that a friend moved to the other side of the country. The practice is to accept that fact.

- A person struggles with the assertion that their potential romantic partner declined a request for a date. The practice is to accept that fact.

The coachee can practice accepting the assertion in a centered body shape or an open body shape, versus their current shape.

THIRTY-
SEVEN

Coaching to the Four Pivot Points

"Change occurs when excuses pivot to execution."
Ryan Lilly[44]

Working with the Four Pivot Points can be powerful and an obvious place for the coach to explore coaching in, with, and through the body. Fundamentally, when working with the pivot points, the goal is to help the coachee either expand, contract, or relax (neither expand nor contract) muscles associated with the pivot points. It is likely that at any given time the coachee has expanded or contracted the pivot point, so the actual practice for them is to simply relax, expand, or contract the pivot point. The practice chosen will be the other end of the spectrum of what the coachee is now doing.

When to Use the Pivot Techniques

Pivot point techniques can be used in many different coaching scenarios. As a coach, the awareness of the pivot points allows for potential suggestions to the coachee about how to better embody one of the basic body shapes, or how to shift their body through only focusing on one to two body areas.

Some simple pivot point practices:

Eyes

- relaxing eyes
- focusing eyes
- centering with eyes open versus closed

Jaw

- jaw relaxing (allow the jaw to hang loosely with teeth not touching)
- jaw tensing (clenching the teeth)

Hands

- hands open (amiable body shape)
- backs of hands (methodical body shape)
- pointing hands (results body shape)
- moving hands (spontaneous body shape)

Feet

- feet flat on ground (centered)
- feet on the balls of the foot
- feet on the heels

Regardless of which is accessed, coaching to the pivot points can be an effective way to create awareness with the coachee about his or her body.

The *Liquid Accordion* in Action

The Haves—and Have Nots—of The Body in Language

We have:
- balls
- lots of gall
- guts
- an eye for detail
- eyes bigger than our stomach
- a green thumb
- cold feet
- itchy feet

We have no:
- guts
- brains
- vision
- balls
- stomach for something
- heart to do something

THIRTY-EIGHT

Coaching to Chakras/ Body Armoring

"Armoring forms different patterns in each person; each of us favors some styles of expression and of holding more than others. In a very real and remarkable way our armoring presents a fossilized history of its own development: old feelings that have turned to stone, layer upon frozen layer, like the rings of some prehistoric tree. It is possible systematically to bring these fossil feelings back to life, liberating the energy that is trapped in holding them down—trapped in the past."

Nick Totten and Em Edmondson,[45] *Reichian Growth Work*

Awareness of Chakras and Body Armoring are paths that can take coaches years to understand and master. For our purposes, as we begin to coach in, with, and thorough the body, we explore them as a way to begin creating awareness of the body and places for the coach to listen and open up new paths to the coachee. The purpose of this book is not to make one a master of either of the disciplines, but rather to provide a place to start.

Because of this, it is the understanding of both disciplines that the coach can use to ensure a grounded assessment of where to offer to take the coaching journey. We group them together since there is a strong correlation between the two. Chakras are about the body energy and tapping into its body wisdom. Body armoring is about blocks of energy in the body. As we have seen, there are seven chakras and seven body armoring locations, all of which fit fairly well together.

The idea for coaching to the Chakras/Body Armoring is that as the coach and coachee become aware of certain regions of the body, the regions themselves may provide places to explore in much deeper ontological/somatic coaching. For the beginning coach, this awareness, among other things, will produce potential directions to lead for further learning and study. This could be as simple as starting to learn more about Chakras and/or Body Armoring.

When to Use the Chakras/Body Armoring Techniques

Chakras/Body Armoring techniques can be used in any coaching situation to bring awareness to the coachee and coach. In practices like the scanner technique, or in somatic role-playing, as the coachee notices that they have sensations, awarenesses, energy, pain—or a lack of any of these—in certain areas of the body, this knowledge can lead to a deeper understanding of what this reality might mean.

I'll provide two examples to further clarify.

Example #1

In the coaching conversation, the coach notices that at certain points in the conversation the coachee seems to "be in their head," and their body seems to be not moving, almost lifeless. The coach also assesses that the coachee has a very methodical body shape in their actions and behaviors.

The coach has a bit of understanding about the ocular band in body armoring and knows that individuals with ocular band armoring tend to be disconnected from their bodies and tend to "be in their heads." This allows the coach to offer a conversation with the coachee about what would be possible if they were to explore the current breakdown from a different body shape, or through doing some activities to get the coachee "out of their head" and into their body. This is not about a diagnosis, but rather for the coach and coachee to possibly find a different way, somatically, to explore the current observer and a new possible future observer.

Example #2

In the coaching conversation, the coach notices that at certain points in the conversation, when it seems the conversation is getting very emotional, the coachee continues to cover and rub their throat with their hands. The coach assesses that the coachee has a very amiable body shape. The coach also assesses that when the coachee speaks while their hands are over their throats, the words are softer and quieter.

The coach, having very little knowledge of Chakras, checks out the Thoracic Chakra page presented earlier in this book and sees that the throat region has to do with the vocal cords. When this Chakra is blocked or deficient there is a "fear of speaking, soft and weak voice, shy . . . inability to convey thoughts and feelings." This awareness helps the coach offer to the coachee a practice of making a declaration in a body shape of results and to focus on speaking more loudly and clearly when they make the declaration. This simple practice might help the coachee create breakthoughs in this aspect of their life.

There are countless ways to coach with an understanding of either the Chakras or Body Armoring. These are simply examples, and this is merely provided as a place to start.

THIRTY-NINE

Somatic Practices and Disciplines

*"Practice isn't the thing you do once you're good.
It's the thing you do that makes you good."*
Malcolm Gladwell[46]

A great way to learn about the body is to practice *in, with, and through the body*. As we become aware of our liquid accordion we can deepen our learning with many different practices to better understand who we are. In this chapter I provide a list of somatic practices that can aid in one's growth and understanding of the body. Many of the practices in somatic coaching are derived from the disciplines on this list. The list is by no means complete and is simply a place to start your journey of exploration of the amazing thing we call the body—in our case, our liquid accordion.

One key thought, though, will serve us well before we get to the list.

The practice itself will create a new shape. Something as simple as weightlifting and exercise will create a new shape as your body adapts to the new practice. This can be both good and bad news.

Good news: the practice can open up the body to new ways of seeing and being in the new shape. This can lead to new awareness and possibilities.

Bad news: any physical discipline can be taken to an extreme, and a new shape can become too rigid. An example is someone who becomes so into a new practice that that practice becomes their new observer. Remember, though, that we have a shape, but we also have an unshape, so we can potentially lose sight of how to be different observers if we take any path too far, to an extreme.

* * * *

Aikido: Aikido is a Japanese form of defensive martial arts that is based on holds and locks and utilizes the principles of nonresistance with an opponent to debilitate and minimize the opponent's strength. Many of the foundational somatic practices in the ontological coaching discourse have Aikido as part of their foundation. Like many martial arts, there are various sub-disciplines that have specific criteria or tenets. A quick search online can provide more resources and potential local dojos for the study of Aikido.

Improv Comedy: Improvisational comedy, or improv, is based on a small group of people working in the domain of comedy and improvising skits based on random ideas and the general vibe occurring at that time. It is a great somatic practice for several reasons. First, improv's fundamental tenet—"yes, and"—is about accepting what the other person provides for you and going with it; second, participants are taught not to think too deeply about an answer but to simply go with what comes to them. This is a great

>> >> >> >> >> >> >> >> >> >> The *Liquid Accordion* in Action

Observing the Liquid Accordion in the Wild: Meeting Time

The next time you are in a meeting, have fun with the liquid accordion that is . . . yourself. Try some of the following and see what shows up for you.

• While in the meeting, sit with your back up, away from your chair, leaning into the meeting. What do you see? How much of an urge do you feel to take action and be in the conversation?

• Next, sit back, *into* your chair and feel the back of the chair entirely with your back and back side. Does the meeting show up differently?

• Now, as you are sitting back in the chair, take your hands and open them, palms up under the table, and keep them open. This can be especially revealing when there is tension in the meeting. What do you notice as your hands are open? Do you have an urge to close them and turn them palms down? If you do, what does the meeting look like then? Experiment with this action and see what shows up for you.

practice to get coachees out of their heads. Many comedy clubs or community colleges offer programs to explore improv.

Exercise, Any Exercise: Sometimes simple exercise, any exercise, can be a great somatic practice. The act of getting active in the body can open up the body. A quick check-in with a coachee to see if they are doing any form of workout or physical activity can determine if simple exercise might be the first practice for the coachee to begin.

Tai Chi: This is a Chinese-based martial art involving slow meditative moves and practices that has strong health, relaxation, and balance benefits. The basic idea is to practice moves slowly to feel and embody them—with the ability to move fast always available for the practitioner. Like many martial arts, there are various sub-disciplines that have specific criteria or tenets. Many communities have Tai Chi centers, and many health organizations have classes as well.

Yoga: Yoga is an ascetic Hindu practice taught through controlled breathing, prescribed body positions, meditation focused on mental and physical well-being, and deep spiritual insights and tranquility. There are various sub-disciplines that have specific criteria or tenets in yoga, each with specific points of focus. Most communities have yoga classes and yoga studios, and many health care systems offer yoga classes.

Breathing: The most fundamental of exercises, breathing has been a practice in many disciplines since the beginning of mankind. From deep breathing to fast, short breaths, there are practices galore for one to study. Many times the breathing exercises will be in tandem with other practices such as yoga, martial arts, and meditation. Many online entities and phone apps have simple breathing exercises to try.

Meditation: Many different practices can fall into meditation, which is fundamentally any practice or exercise which involves both an intellectual/contemplative exercise combined with breathing exercises and relaxation components. Another multi-discipline definition, many discourses define themselves as meditation. Many local organizations, including health care, have meditation practices. There are also many phone meditation apps available.

Mindfulness: Much like meditation and, many times overlapping with it, mindfulness practices are about breaking attention and awareness to the body and the soul/inner being of a person. There are many practices in this discourse, and there are both local and online resources available to learn more and engage.

Massage or Massage Therapy: This is physical manipulation of the soft tissue of the body performed by another for the purpose of normalizing and relaxing those tis-

sues. The masseuse uses their hands and arms, along with tools, to apply pressure and induce the release of tension in the body. Most message therapists must be licensed in some form by a government agency; therefore, one should do research into finding a massage therapist that serves the individual's needs.

Somatic Body Work:
This is a specialized form of somatic coaching bringing together many discourses such as massage, Rolfing (see just below), and reiki to help the coachee release body armoring. The practice is done with both physical manipulation and the wisdom of the somatic practitioner to help the coachee gain awareness in domains of their body where there is numbing body armor. There is specific training for this, and some states require forms of licensing. There is also a strong link to therapy in somatic body work, so it is necessary to do research in this field to ensure practitioners are competent and in good standing.

Trauma/Tension Releasing Exercises (TRE):
TRE is a discipline developed by David Berceli, PhD, to help the body release tension and trauma. It is based on simple exercises and meant to cause certain muscles in the body to reach a point where they shake and release the tension and trauma in the body. It is recommended to seek a licensed practitioner in this field.

Rolfing:
Rolfing is the practice of manipulation of the fascia, the internal webbing that connects all of our internal muscles. Developed by Ida Rolf, it has documented health benefits. Practitioners of Rolfing must be specifically trained and certified; therefore, one needs to do research on the practice and practitioner.

Being Outside: Hiking, Gardening:
A final practice that can have huge somatic benefits is simply being outside and doing things like hiking and gardening. A connection with nature can be a powerful way to connect with the body. Best of all, all one has to do is walk outside.

APPENDIX 1

· · · · · · · · · · · · · · · · · ·

References

I am providing a list of books that have a direct link to somatics and the body. Many of them influenced the writing of this book. Those books which had a large impact on this book are specifically referenced. The books are broken into categories of their main focus.

General Books on Somatics

The following books are mainly about the subject of somatics.

Balsley, Chris. *Stop Controlling Start Leading, 27 Secrets for Effective Leadership at Work, Home, and Play* (2015).

Blake, Amanda. *Your Body is Your Brain, Leverage Your Somatic Intelligence to Find Purpose, Build Resilience, Deepen Relationships, and Lead More Powerfully.* Trokay Press, 2018.

Blakeslee, Sandra, and Blakeslee, Matthew. *The Body Has a Mind of Its Own.* New York, Random House Trade Paperbacks, 2008.

Caldwell, Christine. *Bodyfulness, Somatic Practices for Presence, Empowerment, and Waking Up in This Life.* Shambala (Boulder, CO), 2018.

Dale, Claire and Peyton, Patricia. *Physical Intelligence: Harness Your Body's Untapped Intelligence to Achieve More, Stress Less, and Live More Happily.* London, Random Simon and Schuster, 2019.

Damasio, Antonio. *Descartes' Error, Emotion, Reason, and the Human Brain.* New York, Quill, 1994.

Damasio, Antonio. *The Feeling of What Happens: Body and Emotion in the Making of Consciousness.* Harcourt, Inc. (San Diego, CA), 1999.

Dychtwald, Ken. *BodyMind.* Jeremy P. Tarcher, Inc., Los Angeles, 1986.

Hamill, Pete. *Embodied Leadership: The Somatic Approach to Developing Your Leadership.* Kogan Page (London), 2013.

Hay, Louise. *Heal Your Body, The Mental Causes for Physical Illness and the Metaphysical Way to Overcome Them.* Carlsbad, CA, Hay House, 1988.

Heller, Stuart. *The Dance of Becoming, Living Life as a Martial Art.* Berkely, CA, North Atlantic Books, 1991.

Keleman, Stanley. *Your Body Speaks its Mind.* New York, Pocket Books, 1976.

Keleman, Stanley. *Somatic Reality, Bodily Experience and Emotional Truth.* Berkeley, CA, Center Press, 1979.

Keleman, Stanley. *Emotional Anatomy.* Berkeley, CA, Center Press, 1985. (A foundational book on the physiology of what happens in the body as we, as humans navigate the world. This book is a key book for the foundational underpinnings of Part 1, The Why of Coaching In, With and Through the Body).

Keleman, Stanley. *Embodying Expereince, Forming a Personal Life.* Berkeley, CA, Center Press, 1997.

Keleman, Stanley. *Love, A Somatic View.* Berkeley, CA, Center Press, 1994.

Palmer, Wendy. *The Intuitive Body, Discovering the Wisdom of Conscious Embodiment and Aikido.* Berkeley, CA, Blue Snake Books, 2008.

Lewis, Thomas, Amini, Fari, and Lannon, Richard. *A General Theory of Love.* New York, Vintage Books, 2000.

Palmer, Wendy, and Crawford, Janet. *Leadership Embodiment, How the Way We Sit and Stand Can Change the Way with Think and Speak.* San Rafael, CA, The Embodiment Foundation, 2013.

Palmer, Wendy. *Dragons and Power, Embodying Your Noble, Awesome and Shiny Dragon Spirit.* Berkeley, CA, Wendy Palmer, 2020.

Strozzi-Heckler, Richard. *Aikido and the New Warrior.* Berkeley, CA, North Atlantic Books, 1985.

Strozzi-Heckler, Richard. *Anatomy of Change, A Way to Move Through Life's Transitions.* Berkeley, CA, North Atlantic Books, 1993.

Strozzi-Heckler, Richard. *Holding the Center, Sanctuary in a Time of Confusion.* Berkeley, CA, Frog Books, 1997.

Strozzi-Heckler, Richard. *Being Human at Work, Bringing Somatic Intelligence Into Your Professional Life.* Berkeley, CA, North Atlantic Books, 2003.

Strozzi-Heckler, Richard. *In Search of the Warrior Spirit, Teaching Awareness Disciplines to the Military.* Berkeley, CA, Blue Snake Books, 2007.

Strozzi-Heckler, Richard. *The Leadership Dojo, Build Your Foundation as an Exemplary Leader.* Berkeley, CA, Frog Limited, 2007. (This book had a great influence on the Breath to Blend centering technique in Part 3 of the book, the How of Coaching In, With, and Through the Body.)

Strozzi-Heckler, Richard. *The Art of Somatic Coaching, Embodying Skillful Action, Wisdom and Compassion.* Berkeley, CA, North Atlantic Books, 2014. (Another of Richard Strozzi's books which greatly influenced this book. It is in the book that Strozzi-Heckler outlines his methodology which influenced Chapter 28, The Somatic Arc of Coaching).

Strozzi-Heckler, Richard. *Embodying the Mystery, Somatic Wisdom for Emotional, Energetic and Spiritual Awakening.* Rochester, VT, Inner Traditions, 2022.

Walsh, Mark. *Embodiment- Moving Beyond Mindfulness.* Unicorn Slayer Press, 2020.

Zeman, Suzanne. *Listening to Bodies, A Somatic Primer for Coaches, Managers and Executives.* Richmond, CA, Shasta Gardens Publishing, 2008.

Ontological / Generative Leadership

All of the following books explore the Ontological/ Generative Leadership discourses and the concepts in these books either directly or indirectly deal with somatics and coaching in, with, and through the body.

Brothers, Chalmers, and Kumar, Vinay. *Language and the Pursuit of Leadership Excellence, How Extraordinary Leaders Build Relationships, Shape Culture Drive Breakthrough Results* (2nd ed.). Naples, FL, New Possibilities Press, 2015.

Brothers, Chalmers, *Language and the Pursuit of Happiness, A New Foundation for Designing your Life, Your Relationships & Your Results.* Naples, FL, New Possibilities Press, 2005.

Feltman, Charles. *The Thin Book of Trust, An Essential Primer for Building Trust at Work* (2nd Ed.). Bend, OR, Thin Book Publishing, 2021.

Flores, Fernando. *Conversations For Action and Collected Essays, Instilling a Culture of Commitment in Working Relationships.* North Charleston, SC, CreateSpace Independent Publishing Platform, 2012.

Marsden, Marcus. *Start with Who, Reveal the Hidden Power of Identity to Create a Purposeful Life.* Singapore, Candid Creation Publishing, 2022.

Sieler, Alan. *Coaching to the Human Soul, Volumes 1-4*. Blackburn, Australia, Alan Sieler, 2003, 2007, 2012, 2020. (Volume II has specific ideas relating to the Eight Basic Moods of Life).

Chakras, Body Armoring, and Other Somatic Methodologies

The following books either deal directly or indirectly with specific somatic topics and themes.

Baker, Elsworth. *Man in the Trap, The Causes of Blocked Sexual Energy*. Princeton, NJ, The American College of Orgonomy Press, 2000.

Berceli, David. *Shake it off Naturally, Reduce Stress, Anxiety, and Tension with (TRE)*. David Berceli, 2015.

Brennan, Barbara Ann. *Hands of Light, A Guide to Haling Through the Human Energy Field*. New York, NY, Bantam Books, 1987.

Brennan, Barbara Ann. *Light Emerging, The Journey of Personal Healing*. New York, NY, Bantam Books, 1993.

Dolowich, Gary. *Archetypal Acupuncture, Healing with the Five Elements*. Aptos, CA, Jade Mountain Publishing, 2003.

Frisch, Patricia. *Whole Therapist, Whole Patient, Integrating Reich, Masterson, and Jung in Modern Psychotherapy*. New York, NY, Routledge, 2018.

Judith, Anodea. *Eastern Body, Western Mind, Psychology and the Chakra System asa Path to the Self*. Berkeley, CA, Celestial Arts, 2004.

Nestor, James. *Breathe, The New Science of a Lost Art*. New York, NY, IA, Riverhead Books, 2020.

Reich, Wilhelm. *The Discovery of the Orgone, The Function of the Orgasm*. New York, NY, The Noonday Press, 1961.

Reich, Wilhelm. *Character Analysis,* (Third, Enlarged Edition). New York, NY, The Noonday Press, 1972.

Totton, Nick and Edmundson, *Em. Reichian Growth Work, Melting the Blocks to Life and Love*. Ross-on-Wye, England, PCCS Books, 2009.

Yandell, Judith. *Chakras for Beginners, The Complete Guide to Balancing the 7 Chakras and Healing Your Body with Guided Chakra Meditation*. Judith Yandell, 2019.

Emotions

Ekman, Paul. *Emotions Revealed, Recognizing Faces and Feelings to Improve Communication and Emotional Life*. New York, St. Martin's Griffin, 2003 and 2007.

Newby, Dan and Nunez, Lucy. *The Unopened Gift, A Primer in Emotional Literacy.* Daniel Newby and Lucy Nunez, 2017.

Newby, Dan, and Watkins, Curtis. *The Field Guide to Emotions, A Practical Orientation to 150 Essential Emotions.* Daniel Newby and Curtis Watkins, 2019.

Four Body Shapes / Dispositions / Social Styles and Archetypes

Dealing with the ideas shared in Chapters 11-18 on the Four Plus 1 Basic Body Shapes in The What and Where of Coaching In, With and Through the Body, the following books explore the different shapes.

Arrien, Angeles. *The Four-Fold Way, Walking the Paths of the Warrior, Teacher, Healer and Visionary.* New York, NY, Harper One, 1993.

Bolton, Robert and Bolton, Dorothy. *People Styles at Work, Making Bad Relationships Good and Good Relationships Better.* New York, NY, Amacom 1996.

Collins, David and Myers, John. *Adaptive Selling, How to Succeed During Times of Disruption.* Des Moines, IA, Book Press, 2021.

Jung, C. G. *Four Archetypes.* Princeton, NJ, Princeton University Press, 1969.

Moore, Robert and Gillette, Douglas. *King, Warrior, Magician, Lover, Rediscovering the Archetypes of the Mature Masculine.* San Francisco, CA, HarperSanFranciso, 1990.

Mulqueen, Casey and Collins, David. *Social Style and Versatility Facilitator Handbook.* Centenial, CO, TRACOM Press, 2014.

Myers, John and Pfaffhausen, Henning. *The Versatility Factor, Strategies for Building High-Performing Relationships.* Des Moines IA, Book Press Publishing, 2016.

Reid, Roger. *Personal Styles and Effective Performance.* Boca Raton, FL, CRC Press, 1999.

Wilson Learning. *The Social Styles Handbook, Find Your Comfort Zone and Make People Feel Comfortable with You.* Nova Vista, 2004.

APPENDIX 2

· · · · · · · · · · · · · · · · · ·

Glossary

Assertion: one of the speech acts. Assertions are what we consider factual. They are either true or false, and they can be in the present or past.

Assessment: one of the speech acts. Assessments are our opinions and judgments. They can never be true nor false, but they may be grounded or ungrounded.

Body armor: based on the work of Wilhelm Reich, body armoring is a concept that we as humans have bands (regions of the body), in which the muscles in that band are constricted and tense. This causes a numbing of the emotions associated with that band. This allows us to navigate the world from a certain perspective.

BEL: ontological coaching distinction meaning (B)body, (E)emotions, and (L)language. The BEL makes up our observer. When there is congruence in our BEL, we are in alignment with our cares. A lack of the congruence creates breakdowns for us as observers.

Breakdown: a breakdown is when an unexpected occurrence creates a situation where an observer has to take some form of action to navigate the occurrence. The concept of the breakdown is fundamental to ontological coaching; without a breakdown there cannot be coaching. A key distinction is that only the person to whom the breakdown occurs can declare it a breakdown. What one person sees as a breakdown may not be a breakdown at all for another person.

Break in transparency: a break in transparency is when an unexpected occurrence happens, and although the observer becomes aware of it, it does not cause in the observer a need to take an action to deal with it. When a break in transparency occurs, one person can see it as a breakdown and another not as a breakdown.

Chakra: Chakras are ancient body distinctions which are about the seven primary energy locations in the body. The basic tenet is that when energy flows through the chakra we experience health, energy, and vibrancy, and when the chakras are blocked or hindered we experience emotional and physical breakdowns and health issues.

Declaration: one of the speech acts. A declaration is a statement uttered, either aloud or internally, by someone with the authority to create a new future by the utterance of the declaration. A declaration can be relatively trivial—"I am hungry"—or profound: a judge can declare someone guilty or innocent of an accused crime.

Emotion: a predisposition to action. An emotion is caused by a specific event, which shifts the predisposition we are currently in (another emotion, or a mood), to another, which leads us to be predisposed to take a different action. Emotions tend to live in a shorter period of time.

Mood: a predisposition to action. A mood is an overall predisposition to action which is running in the background of our observer. Moods are generally for longer periods of time than emotions. If we live in an emotional space long enough, it can then become a mood.

OAR: a basic ontological coaching distinction: the (O)observer we are sees (A)actions to take to create (R)results.

Observer: a basic ontological coaching distinction. The observer we are determines how we see and navigate our world. The Observer is made up of our (B)body, (E)emotions, and (L)language.

Offer: one of the speech acts. An offer is to put oneself forward to do something for others.

Promise: one of the speech acts. A promise is a commitment to take specific actions for another person (or ourselves).

Request: one of the speech acts. A request is when we attempt to get others to take some specific action for us.

SELPH: a generative learning distinction. Much like the BEL, the SELPH includes the (B) body, (E)emotions, and (L)language, but uses (S)somatics (replacing "body") and adds in (P)practices and (H)historical discourse.

Speech acts: the six basic linguistic tools we use as humans. They include assertion, assessment, declaration, offer, promise, and request.

Somatics: the living human body in its physicality, shape, and presence as it relates to how an individual perceives, senses, navigates, understands, and interacts with the world around themselves.

Somatic/Ontological/Generative Learning Organizations

Below is a list of some of the organizations that I am aware of and have been influenced by that are somatic/ontological/generative learning organizations. The list is not complete and there are many additional somatic learning organizations which are in alignment with the content of this book.

The Strozzi Institute

- Founded by Richard Strozzi-Heckler, The Strozzi institute is a premier somatic and embodiment training organization. Located in Petaluma, CA, they offer many beginner through advanced somatic coaching and leadership programs, primarily in in-person formats

strozziinstitute.org

The Newfield Network

-Founded by Julio Olalla, The Newfield Network is the premier and foundational ontological coach training organization. Located in Boulder, CO, Newfield offers ontological coach training in both in-person and virtual formats.

Newfieldnetwork.com

The Coach Partnership (TCP)
- Founded by masterful ontological coaches, TCP, located in Singapore, offers ontological and somatic training programs in both virtual and in-person formats based on the Newfield Network ontological coaching methodology. Thecoachpartnership.com

The Institute of Generative Leadership (IGL)
-Founded by Bob Dunham, IGL is the premier Generative Coach training organization. IGL offers graduate level programs in coaching in organizations. Generativeleadership.co

Integral Coaches and the Advanced Coaching Practicum (ACP)
- Founded by Libby Robinson, MCC, an ontological coach, Integral and its ACP program offer ontological and somatic coach training in both virtual and in-person formats. advancedcoachingpracticum.com integralcoaches.com

ABOUT CROFT EDWARDS

Croft Edwards is a Master Certified Coach (MCC) leadership expert and the genesis behind LeadershipFlow, the study of how to help individuals and organizations be at their best. He has been coaching and consulting since 2001. He brings a varied and unique perspective to his clients through his application of leadership from both practical and historical perspectives. Croft's academic training includes business, history, mindfulness, somatic's and other cutting edge coaching methodologies. His practical experience is through military leadership, corporate work, and consulting careers, and as President of CROFT + Company, a leadership and change coaching and consulting firm.

Croft's expertise as a leadership coach is in transformational coaching methodologies of Ontological, Generative and Somatic coaching. He has coached hundreds of leaders and has over 10,000 documented hours as a coach. He currently coaches senior leaders in the US Army, The US Navy and the US Air Force, along with many businesses and government entities as diverse as mines, medical schools, Tech companies, start-ups, and Sovereign nations Croft's formal coaching education is through the Leadership and Coaching Program from Villanova University and the Newfield Network in Ontological Coaching. He is also a graduate of the Coaching Excellence in Organizations (CEO) Program from the Institute of Generative Leadership, and several Somatic's programs with the Strozzi Institute. He is a mentor coach with The Newfield Network, The Coach Partnership, Integral Coach Training, and the Institute of Generative Leadership. His Master Certified Coach designation is from the International Coach Federation (ICF), where Croft is a member in good standing. He has a bachelor's degree in financial administration from Michigan State University, an MBA from Auburn University, and a Masters of Civil War Studies from the American Military University. He is also the author of the book *LeadershipFlow: Perfectly Square, A Story About Learning to Lead and Transforming a Company.*

Croft learned and honed many of his leadership skills in the U. S. Army. He spent over five years on active duty in the U.S. and the Far East and spent over 20 years in the Army National Guard and Army Reserve. The majority of his time in the Army was in leadership positions, including an M1 tank platoon leader in Korea, and a commander of a field artillery battery in the Army National Guard. He also spent many years teaching leadership for the Army as an instructor and Adjunct Professor at the Command and General Staff College at Fort Leavenworth, Kansas.

When not working Croft spends his time with his wife and three daughters on a small farm in New Mexico. His hobbies include farming, woodworking and running.

ENDNOTES

1 by Richard Rodgers, The Sound of Music

2 Strozzi-Heckler, Richard. 2020. Interview by Author. 4 Aug.

3 Dictionary.com. 2021. Accessed 15 July. https://www.dictionary.com/browse/somatic

4 Merriam-Webster. 2023. Accessed 3 October. https://www.merriam-webster.com/dictionary/somatic

5 Cambridge Dictionary. 2023. Accessed 3 Oct. https://dictionary.cambridge.org/dictionary/english/somatic?q=Somatic

6 Dictionary.com. 2023. Accessed 3 Oct. https://www.dictionary.com/browse/embodiment

7 Merriam-Webster. 2023. Accessed 3 October. https://www.merriam-webster.com/dictionary/embodiment

8 Dictionary.com. 2021 Accessed 15 Jul. https://www.dictionary.com/browse/body

9 Merriam-Webster. 2023. Accessed 3 October. https://www.merriam-webster.com/dictionary/embody

10 Cambridge Dictionary. 2023. Accessed 3 Oct. https://dictionary.cambridge.org/dictionary/english/somatic?q=Embody

11 National Geographic. 2013. https://www.nationalgeographic.com/science/article/how-many-cells-are-in-your-body

12 Keleman, Stanley, 1989 Emotional Anatomy, The Structure of Experience. Center Press. P. 5

13 Dychtwald, Ken. 1986 BodyMind. Tarcher Putnam. P. 24.

14 Welch, Raquel .2025. https://www.goodreads.com/search?q=raquel+welch&search%5Bsource%5D=goodreads&search_type=quotes&tab=quotes. accessed 1 May 25.

15 Van der Kolk, Bessel. 2015. The Body Keeps the Score: Brain, Mind, and Body in the Healing of Trauma. Penguin Books. P. 97.

16 American Psychological Association. 2025 https://www.apa.org/topics/trauma/.

17 Psychologytoday.com/us/basics/trauma. Accessed 5 May 2025.

18 Sadhguru (need endnote info). Sadhguru.2014.. Interview by Shekhar Kapur. In Conversation with the Mystic. 5:35. https://www.youtube.com/watch?v=M-V9q5ZemS0&t=3s

19 Murakami, Haruki. Norwegian Wood https://www.goodreads.com/search?q=Haruki+Murakami&search%5Bsource%5D=goodreads&search_type=quotes&tab=quotes. Access 5 May 25.

20 Frisch, Patricia R. 2018. Whole Therapist, Whole Patient: Integrating Reich, Masterson, and Jung in Modern Psychotherapy. Routhledge. P. 30.

21 Totten, Nick and Edmondson, Em. 2009. Reichian Growth Work: Melting the Blocks of Life and Love. PCCS. P. 30.

22 Durckheim, Graf. https://www.goodreads.com/search?utf8=%E2%9C%93&q=Graf+Durckheim+&search_type=quotes. Accessed 4 May 2021.

23 https://www.goodreads.com/search?utf8=%E2%9C%93&q=isadora+duncan+dancing&search_type=quotes. Access 4 May 2021

24 De la Bruyere, Jean. https://www.goodreads.com/search?utf8=%E2%9C%93&q=-Jean+de+la+Bruyere+&search_type=quotes. Accessed 4 May 2021.

25 Mitchell, David. https://www.goodreads.com/search?utf8=%E2%9C%93&q=David+Mitchell+body&search_type=quotes

26 Van Booy, Simon. https://www.goodreads.com/search?utf8=%E2%9C%93&q=simon+van+-booy+hands&search_type=quotes Accessed 4 May 2021.

27 Ueshiba, Morihei, https://www.portsmouthaikido.org/quotes . Accessed 5 May 2025

28 Olalla, Julio. https://www.linkedin.com/posts/joshuadietrich_management-leadership-coaching-activity-7036761515399503872-BIBm/ Accessed 5 May 2025.

29 Kazantzakis, Nikos. https://www.goodreads.com/search?utf8=%E2%9C%93&q=Nikos+Ka-zantzakis+eyes&search_type=quotes, Accessed 4 May 2025.

30 Dictonary.com https://www.dictionary.com/browse/pivot. Accessed 5 May 2025. .

31 Wittgenstein, Ludwig, https://www.goodreads.com/search?utf8=%E2%9C%93&q=Ludwig+Wittgen-stein+human+body&search_type=quotes. Accessed 5 May 2025

32 Replaced this quote with "Stay centered, do not overstretch. Extend from your center, return to your center. -Buddha

33 Yeats, William B. https://www.goodreads.com/search?utf8=%E2%9C%93&q=yeats+body+brain&search_type=quotes. Accessed 5 May 2025.

34 Graham , Martha. https://www.goodreads.com/search?utf8=%E2%9C%93&q=Martha+Graham+body&search_type=quotes. Accessed 5 May 2025.

35 Kenyon, Tom. https://www.azquotes.com/author/57366-Tom_Kenyon. Accessed 5 May 2025.

36 Dychtwald, Ken. 1986 BodyMind. Putnam. P. xvi.

37 Keleman, Stanley, 1989 Emotional Anatomy, The Structure of Experience. Center Press. P. 37

38 Thich Nhat Hang. https://www.goodreads.com/search?utf8=%E2%9C%93&q=Thich+N-hat+Hang+windy+sky&search_type=quotes Accessed 5 May 2025.

39 Schutz, William https://www.azquotes.com/author/19640-William_Schutz. Accessed 5 May 2025.

40 Erwitt, Elliot https://www.azquotes.com/quote/989502 Accessed 5 May 2025.

41 Planck , Max. https://www.goodreads.com/quotes/1246159-when-you-change-the-way-you-look-at-things-the. Acccessed 5 May 2025.

42 Murakami, Haruki. https://kwize.com/quote/11071 Accessed 5 May 2025.

43 Wittgenstein, Ludwig. https://quotation.io/quote/limits-language-means-limits-world. Accessed 5 May 2025.

44 Lilly, Ryan https://www.goodreads.com/quotes/3319489-change-occurs-when-excuses-pivot-to-execution Accessed 5 May 2025.

45 Totten, Nick and Edmondson, Em. 2009. *Reichian Growth Work: Melting the Blocks of Life and Love*. PCCS. P. 60.

46 Gladwell, Malcom. https://www.goodreads.com/work/quotes/3364437-outliers-the-story-of-success. Accessed 5 May 2025.

To learn more, go to the following link where you can purchase more copies of my book using a special discount code:

LiquidAccordion.com

To learn more about Croft Edwards and CROFT + Company, Inc., go to:

Croftandcompany.com